Foreign Language Learning without Vision

Sound Perception,
Speech Production,
and Braille

Takayuki Nakamori

HITUZI
SYOBO

Copyright © Takayuki Nakamori 2016
First published 2016

Author: Takayuki Nakamori

All rights reserved. Except for the quotation of short passages for the purposes of criticism and review, no part of this publication may be reproduced, stored in a retrieval system, or transmitted in any form or by any means, electronic, mechanical, photocopying, recording or otherwise, without the written prior permission of the publisher.
In case of photocopying and electronic copying and retrieval from network personally, permission will be given on receipts of payment and making inquiries. For details please contact us through e-mail. Our e-mail address is given below.

Hituzi Syobo Publishing
Yamato bldg. 2F, 2-1-2 Sengoku Bunkyo-ku Tokyo, Japan 112-0011

phone +81-3-5319-4916 fax +81-3-5319-4917
e-mail: toiawase@hituzi.co.jp
http://www.hituzi.co.jp/
postal transfer 00120-8-142852

ISBN978-4-89476-828-4
Printed in Japan

In memory of Yasui Minoru sensei

Contents

List of Figures   xiii
List of Tables   xv
Preface   xix

Chapter 1   Perception of sounds: music and speech ─────── 1

Introduction   1
1.1. What is sound?   4
   1.1.1. Vibration and frequency   4
   1.1.2. Loudness and timbre   6
1.2. The sound of music   8
   1.2.1. Components of musical sounds   8
   1.2.2. Innateness and responses to sound   11
   1.2.3. Sound and emotions   17
   1.2.4. Music and language   23
1.3. Sounds of human language   31
   1.3.1. Human hearing system   32

1.3.2. Listening to a foreign language   45

1.3.3. Flexibility and plasticity
in the auditory system   49

Chapter 2   Description of English sounds and learning problems —— 55

Introduction   55

2.1. Vowels   56

   2.1.1. High front tense vowel   62

   2.1.2. High front lax vowel   63

   2.1.3. Mid front lax vowel   63

   2.1.4. Low front lax vowel   64

   2.1.5. Low back tense vowel   65

   2.1.6. Mid back vowel   66

   2.1.7. Low back rounded vowel   67

   2.1.8. High back lax vowel   67

   2.1.9. High back tense vowel   68

   2.1.10. Low nonrhotic central vowel   69

   2.1.11. Mid nonrhotic lax central vowel   70

   2.1.12. Front mid-closing diphthong   70

   2.1.13. Central mid-closing diphthong   71

   2.1.14. Front low-closing diphthong   72

   2.1.15. Back low-closing diphthong   73

   2.1.16. Fronting low-closing diphthong   74

   2.1.17. High front centring diphthong   74

   2.1.18. Mid front centring diphthong   75

2.1.19. High back centring diphthong   76
2.2. Consonants   77
   2.2.1. Plosive sounds   82
   2.2.2. Fricative and affricate sounds   86
   2.2.3. Gliding   94
   2.2.4. Context sensitive voicing   98
   2.2.5. Approximant cluster reduction   99
   2.2.6. s cluster reduction   100

Chapter 3   Production of speech: articulatory control   103

Introduction   103
3.1. Voice function   104
   3.1.1. Voice production   105
   3.1.2. Voice and individuals   107
3.2. From perception to production   109
3.3. Intelligibility of speech signals   113
3.4. Articulatory and phonological treatment   117
   3.4.1. Necessity for speech learning   117
   3.4.2. Sound discrimination
        and articulatory skills   119
3.5. Phonological encoding and monitoring   126

Chapter 4 Vision, space representation, and tactile sensation — 133

Introduction   133

4.1. Visual perception   134

   4.1.1. Lightness and brightness   136

   4.1.2. Distance and depth   137

   4.1.3. Objects, faces and motion   138

4.2. Visual and spatial mental representations   140

4.3. Spatial cognition in the blind   143

4.4. Integration of acoustic and optic cues   147

   4.4.1. Vision over audition and audio-visual integration   148

   4.4.2. Talking faces: look and imitate   151

   4.4.3. Identifying location   155

   4.4.4. Detecting and decoding emotional stimuli   156

Chapter 5 Learning of Braille: reading by touch — 161

Introduction   161

5.1. Phonological awareness and English spelling   162

   5.1.1. Literacy and phonological awareness   162

   5.1.2. Complexity of spelling rules   166

5.2. Processing of Braille   169

   5.2.1. Guiding principles   171

   5.2.2. Contractions   172

5.2.3. Transfer   174
5.3. Writing/producing Braille   179
5.4. Cross-modal plasticity   188
5.5. Perceptual limitations and aging   193

Chapter 6   Cognitive and linguistic characteristics   199

Introduction   199
6.1. Concepts and mental representations   200
  6.1.1. What are concepts?   202
  6.1.2. Core cognition and representations   210
  6.1.3. Explicit knowledge and representations   212
6.2. Acquisition of concepts   214
  6.2.1. Overview of cognitive development of the blind   216
  6.2.2. Overview of linguistic development of the blind   224
6.3. Input systems and language processing   233
  6.3.1. Auditory, visual and tactile sensations   234
  6.3.2. Formulaic sequences for accurate and fluent processing   238
  6.3.3. Frequency effects in language learning and processing   240

Chapter 7   Phonological chunking and foreign language learning —— 247

Introduction   247

7.1. Principles of teaching   248

   7.1.1. Position   250

   7.1.2. Presentation   250

   7.1.3. Experience   251

   7.1.4. Expectations   252

   7.1.5. Giving information   252

   7.1.6. Speed   253

7.2. Listening skills   255

7.3. Phonological chunking and communication skills   264

7.4. Tactile skills   277

Chapter 8   Teachers' voices from blind schools in Japan —— 281

Introduction   281

8.1. Background   282

8.2. Teaching reading skills by touch   284

   8.2.1. On the confusion of Japanese and English Braille systems   285

   8.2.2. How to handle unknown words in a text   286

   8.2.3. Sound-letter relationships and Braille   287

- 8.2.4. How to check students' ability of Braille reading   290
- 8.3. Teaching listening skills   291
  - 8.3.1. Use of audio programmes in the classroom   292
  - 8.3.2. Listening to passages or conversations with several paragraphs   293
  - 8.3.3. Braille and listening   294
  - 8.3.4. Time for listening activities   295
  - 8.3.5. Homework   296
  - 8.3.6. Students' reactions to listening activities   297
- 8.4. Teaching speaking skills   298
  - 8.4.1. Teachers' attitudes toward speaking skills   299
  - 8.4.2. Providing a proper balance of the four language skills   301
  - 8.4.3. Necessity of providing speaking instruction   302
  - 8.4.4. Opportunities to interact with native speakers of English   304
- 8.5. Issues in foreign language teaching at blind schools   306
  - 8.5.1. On spelling and Braille   307
  - 8.5.2. On listening and speaking skills   309
  - 8.5.3. On teaching blind children English   311
  - 8.5.4. Teacher's roles   316
  - 8.5.5. Final comments   318

Concluding Remarks — 321
References — 323
Index — 351

List of Figures

Figure 5-1: Japanese Braille code (Reprinted by permission from RNIB)   176

Figure 5-2: English Braille (Reprinted by permission from Duxbury Systems, Inc.)   177

Figure 8-1: Number of years taught at blind schools   283

Figure 8-2: Number of years taught at other schools   284

Figure 8-3: Explain rules for sounds and spelling by phonics   287

Figure 8-4: Touch Braille and pronounce   288

Figure 8-5: Spell by Braille and pronounce   288

Figure 8-6: Spell by Braille after listening to sounds   289

Figure 8-7: Spell by Braille via translation   289

Figure 8-8: Read out Braille text   290

Figure 8-9: Frequency of the use of sound materials   292

Figure 8-10: Listening training with longer texts   293

Figure 8-11: Instruction time for listening   295

Figure 8-12: Listening ability of longer texts   297

Figure 8-13: Necessity of listening and speaking skills   300

Figure 8-14: Time for the four language skills   301

Figure 8-15: Possibility of providing listening and speaking instruction   303

Figure 8-16: Frequency of visits by native speakers   305

List of Tables

Table 1-1: Relationships between physical and perceptual variables   7
Table 1-2: Levels of sequential processing   11
Table 1-3: Musical development and age   15
Table 1-4: Sound and emotions   20
Table 1-5: Schematic of the left and right hemispheres   27
Table 1-6: Hypothesised organisation of musical and linguistic structures   29
Table 1-7: Sound properties analysed by spectrograph   40
Table 1-8: Difficulties in foreign language sound processing   46
Table 2-1: Typical formant values for /i/   62
Table 2-2: Typical formant values for /ɪ/   63
Table 2-3: Typical formant values for /ɛ/   64
Table 2-4: Typical formant values for /æ/   65
Table 2-5: Typical formant values for /ɑ/   66
Table 2-6: Typical formant values for /ɔ/   66

Table 2-7: Typical formant values for /ɒ/ 67

Table 2-8: Typical formant values for /ʊ/ 68

Table 2-9: Typical formant values for /u/ 69

Table 2-10: Typical formant values for /ʌ/ 69

Table 2-11: Typical formant values for /ə/ 70

Table 2-12: Typical formant values for /eɪ/ 71

Table 2-13: Typical formant values for /əʊ/ 72

Table 2-14: Typical formant values for /aɪ/ 73

Table 2-15: Typical formant values for /aʊ/ 73

Table 2-16: Typical formant values for /ɔɪ/ 74

Table 2-17: Typical formant values for /ɪə/ 75

Table 2-18: Typical formant values for /ɛə/ 76

Table 2-19: Typical formant values for /ʊə/ 77

Table 2-20: Acoustic correlates of consonantal features 81

Table 2-21: The consonants of English 82

Table 2-22: Examples of error patterns of fricatives 93

Table 2-23: Examples of error patterns of gliding 98

Table 2-24: Examples of error patterns of voicing 99

Table 2-25: Examples of error patterns of approximant cluster reduction 100

Table 2-26: Examples of error patterns of s cluster reduction 101

Table 3-1: Voice and its characteristics 108

Table 3-2: Error categories and intelligibility 116

Table 3-3: Steps for pronunciation learning 118

Table 4-1: Acoustic cues and emotions   158
Table 5-1: Learning to read written forms   174
Table 5-2: Braille for foreign languages   179
Table 5-3: From reading to spelling   182
Table 6-1: Forms of representations   203
Table 6-2: Theories of concepts   208
Table 6-3: Concepts and blind children   224
Table 6-4: Possibly affected aspects of development   230
Table 6-5: Components of fluency   241
Table 7-1: Listening skills for communication   259
Table 7-2: Development of listening skills   263
Table 7-3: Three-level message analysis   264
Table 7-4: Attaining listening skills for communication   269
Table 7-5: Attaining speaking skills for communication   275
Table 8-1: Planning cycle for better learning and teaching   306
Table 8-2: Types of knowledge and skills to be an effective teacher   317

Preface

At the very end of my previous book, *Chunking and Instruction: The Place of Sounds, Lexis, and Grammar in English Language Teaching*, published in 2009, I wrote:

> How do auditory and visual systems relate to each other in foreign language processing? The relationships between listening and reading, while paying attention to sound processing and letter processing, should be investigated (page 254).

The motivation for this book is to answer this question. Research on multisensory processing, i.e. auditory, visual, and tactile processing, has developed rapidly from the perspectives of brain and cognitive sciences. While I focused on the central processing system as lexical and syntactic processors in my previous book, this book investigates how foreign language learners perceive input and produce output, with special reference to blind people who do not depend on vision. By definition, I am blind myself, and I have been interested in how blind people process and acquire language without one important sensory modality, vision. I will discuss the implications for foreign language learning and teaching for the blind as well as normal-sighted people based on theoretical foundations.

    The organisation of this book is as follows: Chapter 1 defines 'sound' first, and then discusses how the ability to hear is acquired and activated daily, summarises recent findings on the processing of music and language, and focuses on the way foreign language learners develop their listening ability after a certain age. Chapter 2 has a close look at vowels and consonants of English and at the learning problems some native and foreign language learners encounter when acquiring/learning the sound system. Chapter 3 explains how humans produce linguistic sounds with articulators, reviews research on the relationships between speech perception and production, and summarises the implications for speech training. Chapter 4 reviews recent research on vision, imagery, spatial cognition and compensatory mechanisms for the lost sensory modality. Chapter 5 focuses on how blind people learn reading skills by touch, the barriers they encounter when learning Braille, and the interrelationships between sensory modalities: auditory, visual, and tactile sensations. Chapter 6 looks closely at the cognitive and linguistic development of visually impaired learners. Chapter 7 discusses implications for foreign language learning by visually impaired students. The key to success is the attainment of phonological chunking skills. This chapter is closely related to Chapter 8, in which I report on the raw data compiled by the Japanese government concerning the teaching of English in Japanese secondary schools for the blind on the basis of questionnaires and interviews conducted in schools for the blind. As I mentioned before, please note that this book focuses on input and output systems, and not on the central system, which pertains to syntactic, semantic, and pragmatic processing, the main topics of my previous book.

Key terms which are frequently used in this book and their definitions are as follows: *First language* is the language acquired from birth, regardless of the speaker's current proficiency. *Second language* is the language acquired after early childhood (ages 1–3 years) following the first language. *Second language learners* are speakers who are learning the second language in an environment where it is used as a native language by the majority of the speakers (e.g. Japanese students learning English in Britain), while *foreign language learners* are speakers who are learning a language in the classroom, outside of the environment where it is used as a native language by the majority of speakers (e.g. Japanese students learning English in Japan) (Pavlenko, 2014: 22).

As Best (1992) clearly states, in talking about people with visual impairment, we are concerned with a heterogeneous group of people who not only have a range of personalities, psychological makeups and interests, but also have wide-ranging types and degrees of visual impairment. Totally blind people are one of a small subgroup of the visually impaired. Those with total congenital blindness form less than twenty percent of the total population of people with visual impairment.

Regarding the widely used Braille codes at bind schools in Japan, students first learn Japanese Braille in primary schools, and then learn English Braille at secondary schools. This suggests that blind students have to learn English Braille at the same time as learning the English language. It is no wonder that students find it extremely difficult to learn English Braille at the same time as learning English as a foreign language. I propose that it would be far more useful to teach them English as a language first, i.e. in terms of the meanings of words and sentences to a reasonable level of proficiency, and to start to teach them how English words are spelt, namely, in terms of single characters for successive sounds that constitute English words, and to start on English Braille only after they have mastered the sounds of English letters in words before they are introduced to the tactual Braille characters for the sounds of which English words consist. I can see no reason why blind learners cannot be taught the English language verbally first, before being introduced to the tactile Braille characters that symbolise the consecutive sounds in English words.

Finally, I hope that this book will be read by visually impaired colleagues. The Royal National Institute of Blind People (RNIB) recommends a clear font style, such as Arial, Tahoma or Tiresias, in 14-point size. Typesetting of this book is Arial font in 14 point for their accessibility.

Many people have encouraged me, made helpful comments and suggestions, and supported my research project. In alphabetical order, I would like to express my gratitude to the following: Mr Michael Ashby, Professor Martin Ball, Professor Hideo Hayashibe, Dr Ryo Kitada, Professor Susanna Millar, Professor Norihiro Sadato, Dr Kimiko Shimazoe, Professor Neil Smith, Mr Yoshihiro Tanaka, Professor Kiyotada Tazaki, and Professor Minoru Yasui. I acknowledge that English teachers at blind schools all over Japan kindly provided me with data and comments from their students, without which this research project could not have been completed. Members of the Kyoto University Braille Society helped me with encoding and decoding the Braille version of the questionnaire. I am really grateful that members of the committee at the Japan Society for the Promotion of Science and the Japanese Ministry of Education have fully supported me financially for three years. This research project was supported by a Grant-in-aid for Scientific Research (Challenging Exploratory Research 25590284) and a Grant-in-Aid for Publication of Scientific Research Results. Lastly, I would like to thank my parents sincerely for their love and support.

December 2015
Takayuki NAKAMORI, Ph.D.

Chapter 1

Perception of sounds: music and speech

Introduction

It is common to observe that humans are visual creatures. Our reliance upon vision is apparent in the way we navigate and react to our surroundings. We fumble in the dark and instinctively turn to look at the sources of sounds. Visual information also occupies a privileged epistemic role and our language frequently reflects a tight coupling of seeing with knowing in English (Nudds & O'Callaghan, eds., 2009: 1).

We are reminded of the importance of vision whenever we close our eyes or when all the lights go off in the event of a sudden power failure, because what we sense and know about our environment is suddenly gone. In contrast, most people never receive such reminders of the significance of hearing. Our ears are always open and we can hear perfectly well even in the dark (Wolfe, et al., 2012: 243).

However, Handel (1989: xi) cites Helen Keller's reflection on the profoundness of being deaf. According to her, listening put her in the world: listening gave her a sense of emotion, a sense of movement, and a sense of being there that was missing when she was looking. She was more frightened by thunder than by lightning, even though she knew that thunder was harmless and lightning was deadly. She felt far more isolation living with earplugs than living with blinders. Listening is centripetal: it pulls us into the world. Looking is centrifugal: it separates us from the world. She felt audition was more crucial for existence than vision.

Then Handel asks: "If you had to choose, would you prefer to be deaf or blind? Without taking time to reflect, most of us prefer to be deaf, to see rather than hear." He continues: "Now imagine going about your day-to-day life deaf or blind. Blind individuals make it. They communicate, laugh, and joke with blind and sighted people, or they listen to music and so on. However, deaf individuals make it only with extreme difficulty and are generally restricted to the friendship of other deaf individuals. They are cut off from others; they are isolated." For instance, Marschark et al. (eds.)

(2015) discuss a wide spectrum of issues surrounding bilingual deaf. In our culture, Handel claims that he would much prefer to be blind than to be deaf. (Actually, as a blind person, I am wondering why those who have no physical defect occasionally talk lightly about disability like this.) Those parts of human experience that are primarily auditory include the perception of an object's location in space by sound alone; the perception of non-speech sounds, particularly music; and the perception of speech.

There are lots of acclaimed blind musicians in the world, most of whom play without music by ear and from memory. They can reproduce sounds of music accurately when they hear them. Of course, sighted people possess this ability, but it has been said that blind people have very sensitive ears to survive. They live active lives despite the various hardships they may face.

In this chapter, we will define what sounds are, discuss how they are acquired and processed, and investigate the way foreign language learners develop their listening ability after a certain age. We will see the flexibility and plasticity in auditory skills in learning a foreign language. Since visually impaired people develop sensitive auditory mechanisms and articulatory functions without vision, sighted and blind people are not distinguished in Chapters 1–3.

1.1. What is sound?

Intuitively, sounds are public objects of auditory perception. Sounds are what we hear during episodes of genuine hearing (Nudds & O'Callaghan, eds., 2009: 26). To put it more scientifically, according to Everest & Pohlmann (2009: 1), sound can be viewed as a wave motion in air or other elastic media. In this case, sound is a stimulus. Sound can also be viewed as an excitation of the hearing mechanism, which results in the perception of sound. In this case, sound is a sensation.

1.1.1. Vibration and frequency

The essence of sound is the propagation of energy into a medium, usually the air. This energy is transmitted as a pressure wave. The vibration of an object acts on the air molecules surrounding it, compressing those immediately in contact with the vibrating object (Tan, et al., eds., 2010: 9).

The basis of all sound is vibration. The rate at which a particular vibration occurs is frequency. A vibrating object's frequency is the number of cycles in a designated amount of time. For the range of vibration frequencies that produce audible sound, the second is the most logical amount of time to employ in measurement. Cycles per second are referred to as Hertz (Hz).

Most sound sources involve a vibrating object of some kind. Regular vibration produces sound waves that repeat over time. Within a certain range of repetition rates, we perceive the periodic sound wave as being associated with pitch. The perceptual experience of pitch is related to the frequency of vibration in sounds. The ability to perceive pitch relies on the ear's ability to encode frequencies from physical stimuli. In general, the greater the frequency, the higher the pitch.

The pitches that most human beings can detect range from about 20 to 20,000 Hz. This capacity varies widely from person to person, and declines with age. After age 30 or 40, hearing loss associated with aging results in a loss of sensitivity in the higher ranges (Tan, et al., 2010: 32).

The ear is sufficiently sensitive to separate out the different frequency components of a sound. One of the first things the auditory system does is to separate out the different frequency components of the incoming sound on the basilar membrane. The basilar membrane performs a partial analysis of the sound with each place on the basilar membrane being most sensitive to a different frequency component.

The auditory system has several hundred different spectral sensitivities. The auditory system extracts quite detailed information about the spectral composition of sounds. Auditory objects are characterised mainly by their spectra and by the way their spectra change over time. For instance, different vowel sounds in speech can be identified by the positions of their spectral peaks. Similarly, different musical instruments can be identified by the spectral distribution of their harmonics (Plack, 2014: 78).

1.1.2. Loudness and timbre

Particular sounds are events. Sounds take time and involve change; at a minimum they begin and usually they end. A number of qualitatively different stages or a single tone of uniform loudness may compose a sound. The sounds are events in which a medium is disturbed or changed or set into motion in a wave-like way by the motions of bodies. Events such as collisions and vibrations of objects cause the sound events (Nudds & O'Callaghan, eds., 2009: Chapter 2).

The auditory system is very sensitive to differences in the energy of input, that is, in the amplitude of the physical sound wave. Intensity is a function of the amount of power in a sound. It is defined as the amount of power passing through a unit area. Loudness is the sound's apparent strength or magnitude. The more energetic the pressure wave, that is, the greater its amplitude, the louder will be the sound heard as the wave impacts on the ear.

Timbre is that attribute of auditory sensation whereby a listener can judge that two steady-state tones having the same pitch and loudness are dissimilar. In other words, two sounds are different but their pitch and loudness are identical. This allows us to distinguish between a cello and trumpet playing the same tune.

Table 1-1. Relationships between physical and perceptual variables

Physical	Perceptual	Property
frequency (Hz)	pitch	tonal (low – high)
amplitude (dB)	loudness	dynamic (silent – loud)
signal shape (wave form)	timbre	tone quality
time	duration	rhythm, tempo

1.2. The sound of music

In Section 1.1, we had a brief look at some crucial features of sounds. In this section, the processing of musical sounds is clarified, and a comparison with speech sound is made.

1.2.1. Components of musical sounds

All of the different frequency components that make up all the different sounds that are being heard are represented by one physical position of the eardrum at any given instant in time. The time level of event fusion is the point at which trains of vibrations from the air are perceptually categorised according to their frequency and loudness. Individual fibres in the inner ear are tuned to respond to a relatively narrow range of frequencies. A basic analysis is performed on incoming sound in terms of frequency and loudness, the results of which persist briefly as echoic memory (Snyder, 2000: 123).

Once acoustical vibrations are fused into events, they are organised on a higher level into sequences. One aspect of these sequences is melody, defined as any sequence of acoustical events that contains recognisable patterns of contour (high and low) in the time dimension with perceptible pitch-like intervals between successive events. They may be any kinds of sounds that can be recognisable when organised into a relationship of higher and lower, and that sound similar enough to form a unified horizontal sequence (Snyder, 2000: 134). Musical pitch is one of the most salient perceptual aspects of a sound, defined as the property of a sound that enables it to be ordered on a scale going from low to high.

A tone, a periodic sound that elicits a pitch sensation, encompasses the vast majority of musical sounds. Tones can be either pure sinusoidal variations in air pressure at a single frequency, or complex. A sinusoid, also called a sine wave, describes a particular relationship between displacement and time. Displacement simply means the distance an object moves, and a sine wave describes the continuous, regular back and forth displacement of a vibrating object.

Complex tones can be divided into two categories: harmonic and inharmonic. Harmonic complex tones are periodic, with a repetition rate known as the fundamental frequency, and are composed of a sum of sinusoids with frequencies that are all integer multiples, or harmonics, of the fundamental frequency. Inharmonic complex tones are composed of multiple sinusoids that are not simple integer multiples of any common fundamental frequency. Most musical instrumental and vocal tones are more or less harmonic, but some can be inharmonic (Deutsch, ed., 2013: 1).

Timbre has two broad characteristics that contribute to the perception of music. Firstly, it has multitudinous perceptual attributes, some of which are continuously varying, others of which are discrete or categorical. Secondly, it is one of the primary perceptual vehicles for the recognition, identification, and tracking over time of a sound source and thus is involved in the absolute categorisation of a sounding object (Deutsch, ed., 2013: 35).

The actual patterns of time intervals are rhythmic groupings. A larger time interval in the ongoing flow of events will usually form a rhythmic grouping boundary. In a melody consisting of pitches, the pitch intervals form the ups and downs of a contour. An interval moving upward to a higher frequency serves to increase intensity, while an interval moving downward to a lower frequency serves to decrease intensity.

Rhythm can move through time intervals that are longer/slower and shorter/faster. The slower parts of the rhythm are the lower parts of the contour that release tension, and the faster parts of the rhythm are the higher parts of the contour that generate tension.

Finally, the following table summarises the memory systems that process musical sounds:

Table 1-2. Levels of sequential processing

Echoic memory	Short-term memory	Long-term memory
Event fusion: Units formed by change in frequency of vibration, loudness level, or timbre	**Melodic grouping:** Units formed by breaks in pitch contour **Rhythmic grouping:** Units formed by longer duration, higher intensity, etc.	**Formal sectioning:** Units formed by changes in overall shape and patterning

(Snyder, 2000: 35)

1.2.2. Innateness and responses to sound

Every human infant is born into a world with two distinct sound systems. The first is linguistic, which includes the vowels, consonants, and pitch contrasts of the native language. The other is musical, which includes the timbres and pitches of the culture's music. Even without explicit instruction, most infants develop into adults who are proficient in their native language and who enjoy music.

It is becoming increasingly clear that every human being has a biologic guarantee of musicianship. Genetic instructions create a brain and body that are predisposed to be musical. Just as we are born to be linguistic, so we are born with the means to be responsive to music (Hodges, ed., 1996: 42). As we all know, we can sing the melody of music fairly accurately, though it is nearly impossible for us to repeat linguistic sounds of unfamiliar languages.

Lerdahl & Jackendoff (1983: 281) argue that, to the degree that the listener's knowledge is complex and abstract with respect to the musical surface, it becomes more difficult to explain one's acquisition of this knowledge on the basis of simple generalisation over presented musical surfaces. The listener hears pitch events in the context of rhythmic units composed of a contribution of metrical and grouping time spans.

The rules of music correspond closely to principles unconsciously known and used by the experienced listener. One does not have to learn all the rules from scratch; rather, one has no choice about much of it.

Many aspects of the rules are simply the only ways that one's mental abilities make available for organising a musical signal. Much of the complexity of musical intuition is not learned but is given by the inherent organisation of the mind determined by the human genetic inheritance.

It is well known that the left hemisphere of the brain subserves specialised linguistic features, and that the right hemisphere is implicated in musical perception. However, recent scientific research has shown that in musically naïve listeners the right hemisphere seems to be dominant for certain tasks of melodic perception, whereas in musically experienced listeners the left hemisphere is dominant. The rule-based perceptual ability of music is localised in the left hemisphere, the same place as phonological functions.

Studies of very young babies (up to one week of age) suggest that any sound is more calming than no sound at all, and they can discriminate between sounds on the basis of numerous acoustic cues, particularly intensity and frequency. Low frequency tones have a greater calming effect on crying than do tones of higher frequencies, and matched pairs of ascending and descending tonal sequences have a distinct arousing effect.

Somewhere between three and six months, babies start to respond actively to music. They begin to turn towards the source of the sound and to show manifest pleasure and astonishment. Soon after this, music consistently produces bodily movements, often rhythmic swaying or bouncing. Around the age of one year, infants begin to treat new melodies or tone sequences as familiar if these sequences have the same melodic contour and frequency range as a previously heard sequence and as novel if either the contour or range differs.

Absolute pitch or perfect pitch is the ability to correctly identify the musical name or frequency of a given tone or to produce a specified tone without reference to any other objective anchor tone. On the other hand, most musicians and musically experienced people possess a good sense of relative pitch. They have developed an internally consistent scale of pitch that accurately represents the relationships between the 12 semitones of the Western tonal scale.

It is now widely known that pitch representations may be strongest in the very young. Absolute pitch acquisition depends obligatorily on musical exposure and training between the ages of three and six. With increasing age, the salience of this ability gives way to the ability to process and store the overall shape and tonality of a tune; hence, absolute to relative pitching. The mastery of pitch and contour is largely accomplished by the end of the preschool period, and the main features of melodic development in later childhood are those concerned with the accurate representation of pitch-interval relationships, that is, with the formal characteristics of the tonal system (Deutsch, ed., 2013: Chapter 5).

Table 1-3. Musical development and age

Ages	Characteristics
0–1	Reacts to sounds
1–2	Spontaneous music making
2–3	Begins to reproduce phrases of songs heard
3–4	Conceives general plan of a melody Absolute pitch may develop if learns an instrument
4–5	Can discriminate register of pitches Can tap back simple rhythms
5–6	Understands louder/softer Can discriminate same from different in easy tonal or rhythm patterns
6–7	Improved singing in tune Tonal music perceived better than atonal
7–8	Appreciates consonance vs. dissonance
8–9	Rhythmic performance tasks improved

9–10	Rhythmic perception improves Melodic memory improves Two-part melodies perceived Sense of cadence
10–11	Harmonic sense becoming established Some appreciation for finer points of music
12–17	Increase in appreciation, cognitively and in emotional response

(Hargreaves, 1986: 61)

Many different aspects of auditory processing and perception are shaped by experience. It is generally accepted that the potential for plasticity declines with age, but the fully mature auditory system shows considerable adaptive plasticity that can be demonstrated over multiple timescales (Schnupp, Nelken & King, 2011: Chapter 7). Anybody can listen to unfamiliar music of a different culture and sing its melody afterwards. Similarly, it is true that phoneticians, phonologists, and speech therapists as well as antholopologists are able to distinguish and record accurately the variety of sounds in human languages after ear training, even though they have not heard these sounds in their daily lives.

1.2.3. Sound and emotions

Bodily responses are observable common experiences to sound and music. People's heads are nodding, their feet are tapping, or their bodies are swaying. The experience of hearing sounds or listening to music involves highly complex interactions among cognitive, affective and bodily processes that take place within a personal, social and cultural context. The tempo of music played in a restaurant affects drinking behaviour: loud music in a pub makes you drink more (Bacci & Melcher, eds., 2013: Chapter 11). Physical responses include effects on the following: heart or pulse rate; skin conductivity; blood pressure; biochemical responses; respiration; finger, peripheral skin or body temperature; muscular tension and chills; blood volume; and gastric motility (Hallam, et al., 2009: Chapter 11; Koelsch, 2012: Chapter 12).

Both music and language have the quality of expressive phrasing. This refers to how the acoustic properties of both spoken utterances and musical phrases can be modulated to convey emphasis and emotion. Although the content of language can be used to express emotion, it is subservient to the prosody, while emotional expression is more central to music than to language. Emotions are fundamentally important to thought and behaviour as they provide a guide to action. Psychologists have attempted to identify the specific emotions, including affective feelings, moods and passions, expressed by tonal tensions within a piece of music and how such emotions are moderated by volume, rhythm, tempo and pitch (Bacci & Melcher, eds., 2013: Chapter 17; Hallam, et al., 2009: Chapters 12 & 13; Mithen, 2006: Chapter 7; Nussbaum, 2007: Chapters 5 & 6; Tan, et al., 2010: Chapter 14).

It is important to note that rhythm is a fundamental life process. Human beings live in what we perceive to be a rhythmic environment, based on periodicities, including seasons of the year, phases of the moon, daylight, and body operations. Hearing is a primary sense through which we create a stable inner world of time. Sound events occurring across time must be ordered to become meaningful. Some aspects of rhythmic- and time-ordered behaviour are just as true of speech as they are of music (Hodges, ed., 1996: 45).

Focusing a bit more on the linguistic side, naturalistic connected speech is quasi-rhythmic as an acoustic signal. This temporal regularity in speech occurs at multiple timescales. For speech produced at a natural rate, the modulation spectrum across languages peaks between 4 – 6 Hz. These energy modulations correspond in time roughly to the syllable structure or syllabic chunking of speech. The syllabic structure is perceptually critical because it signals the speaking rate, it carries stress and tonal contrasts, and the syllable can be viewed as the carrier of the linguistic and affective prosody of an utterance (Arbib, ed., 2013: Chapter 9). Two types of prosody are usually distinguished as follows (Kemmerer, 2015: Chapter 7):

1. **Emotional prosody** encompasses all the ways in which intonation can be modulated to convey feelings (anger, fear, happiness, sadness, etc.) and attitudes (dominance, politeness, sarcasm, sympathy, etc.).
2. **Linguistic prosody** encompasses all the ways in which intonation can be modulated to signal linguistic distinctions in three different domains: syntactic, lexical and tonal.

The following table depicts the relationships between sound and emotions:

Table 1-4. Sound and emotions

Tempo, note density	• Perceived beat or pulse rate is considered the most decisive. • Fast tempo may be associated with expressions of activity or excitement, happiness, joy, pleasantness, potency, surprise, flippancy, whimsicality, anger, uneasiness and fear. • Slow tempo may be associated with expressions of calmness, serenity, peace, sadness, dignity, solemnity, tenderness, longing, boredom and disgust.
Mode, key	• The major mode is happy, merry, joyful, graceful, serene, solemn and playful. • The minor mode is sad, dreamy, dignified, tensed, disgusted, sentimental and angry.
Loudness	Loud sounds may be associated with expressions of intensity, power, excitement, tension, anger and joy, soft sounds with softness, peace, tenderness, sadness and fear.
Timbre, spectrum	• Tones with many higher harmonics may suggest potency, anger, disgust, fear, activity or surprise. • Tones with few, low harmonics may be associated with pleasantness, boredom, happiness or sadness. • Tones with supressed higher harmonics may suggest tenderness and sadness.

Pitch	• High pitch may be associated with expressions of happiness, gracefulness, serenity, dreaminess, excitement, surprise, potency, anger, fear and activity. Low pitch may suggest sadness, dignity, solemnity, vigour, excitement, boredom and pleasantness. • Large pitch variation may be associated with happiness, pleasantness, activity or surprise, small pitch variation with disgust, anger, fear or boredom.
Intervals	Large intervals sound more powerful than small ones; the octave is perceived as positive and strong, and minor second as the saddest interval.
Melody	• Wide melodic range may be associated with joy, whimsicality, uneasiness and fear, narrow range with expressions of sadness, dignity, sentimentality, tranquillity, delicacy and triumph. • Ascending melody may be associated with dignity, serenity, tension, happiness, fear, surprise, anger and potency. Descending melody may be associated with expressions of excitement, gracefulness, vigour, sadness, boredom and pleasantness. • Stepwise motion may suggest dullness, intervallic leaps excitement; stepwise motion leading to melodic leaps may suggest peacefulness.

Harmony	Complex dissonant harmonies are agitated, exciting, tensed, angry, unpleasant and vigorous and inclined toward sadness, while simple consonant harmonies are happy, gay, relaxed, graceful, serene, dreamy, dignified, serious, majestic and lyrical.
Tonality	Melodies composed to sound joyful, dull and peaceful are tonal, while angry melodies could be atonal. Sad and angry melodies use chromatic harmony.
Rhythm	• Regular or smooth rhythm may be perceived to express happiness, dignity, majesty and peacefulness; irregular or complex rhythm may express amusement, uneasiness and anger. • Varied rhythm may express joy. • Firm rhythms are sad, vigorous and dignified, while flowing rhythms are happy, gay, graceful, dreamy, serene and tender.
Articulation	Staccato may be associated with gaiety, energy, activity, fear and anger, legato with sadness, tenderness, solemnity, longing and softness.
Pauses	Perception of rests is dependent on musical context. Silences following tonal closure are identified more quickly and perceived as less tense than silences following music lacking such closure.

Musical form	• High melodic, harmonic or rhythmic complexity is associated with tension or sadness, low complexity with relaxation, joy or peace. • High complexity with low dynamism may express melancholy depression; high complexity combined with high dynamism may express anxiety and aggressiveness. • Low complexity and average dynamism may be associated with positive emotions. • Repetition, condensation, sequential development and pauses may mean increased tension.

1.2.4. Music and language

The past fifteen years have witnessed an increasing interest in the comparative study of music and language as cognitive systems. Music and language are uniquely human traits, so this interest spans all branches of cognitive science, including anthropology, computer science, education, linguistics, neuroscience, and psychology (Rebuschat, et al., eds., 2012).

The neuroscience of music and language is an area that has received considerable attention over the past decade. It has been hypothesised that music and language involve domain-specific representations, and when similar cognitive processes are conducted on these representations, the brain shares neural resources between the two domains (Rebuschat, et al., eds., 2012: Chapters 22 & 27).

The medical case histories described in Mithen (2006: Chapters 2–5) indicate that the neural networks that process music and language have some degree of independence from each other. It is possible to lose or never to develop one of them while remaining normal in respect to the other, or one can acquire or be born with a deficit in one specific area of music or language processing but not in others, which requires us to consider music and language as separate cognitive domains.

More recently, Higgins (2012: 78) claims that patients with amusia (the loss of certain musical abilities) due to brain lesions do not necessarily develop aphasia (the inability to speak), nor do those with aphasia necessarily develop amusia. This suggests neurological dissociability of the two systems. The two modes seem to involve separate brain areas, even if there is considerable overlap in the areas engaged.

Both music and language have a hierarchical structure, being constituted by acoustic elements (tones or words) that are combined into phrases (melodies or utterances), which can be further combined to make musical events or discourse. The musical aspects of language include melodic contour, timbre variations, and rhythm.

Sloboda (1985) has undertaken a detailed comparison from a cognitive psychological viewpoint, referring to musical phonology (the characterisation of basic sound units), syntax (the rules governing the combination of these units), and semantics (the meanings associated with sequences of these units). For example, originated by Lerdahl & Jackendoff (1983), the perception of a melody might be explained in the same way as the linguistic explanation of a sentence. There are musical equivalents of structures of language such that musical elements and the hierarchical rules for their combination and processing are stored in memory (Hargreaves, 1986: 10).

One of the outcomes of the mother-infant dyad is that the baby becomes motivated to recognise and respond to sound patterns that will later become necessary for speech perception. When parents communicate with their infants, their baby talk naturally emphasises the melodic, timbral, and rhythmic aspects used in the native tongue (Hodges, ed., 1996: 46). The general character includes a higher overall pitch, a wider range of pitch, longer hyper-articulated vowels and consonants, shorter phrases, and greater repetition than are found in speech directed to older children and adults. Mithen (2006: Chapter 6) claims that we talk like this because human infants are born musical and demonstrate an interest in, and sensitivity to, the rhythms, tempos, and melodies of speech long before they are able to understand the meanings of words. In essence, the usual rhythmic and melodic features of spoken language, prosody, are highly exaggerated so that our utterances adopt an explicitly musical character. He suggests that the neural networks for language are built upon or replicate those for music.

In the 1990s, neurological experiments reported three important results. First, they documented the existence of a distributed neural network that incorporates specialised nodal regions for processing sensory and motor aspects of music, as is the case for language. Second, in some cases, cortical areas that underlie musical activities have been shown to be next to, and partly overlap with, those engaged similar language tasks. Thirdly, portions of certain areas are differentially activated in the left hemisphere during specific musical activities. The right temporal association cortex (area 22) is recruited on first hearing a piece of music. In particular, the right hemisphere attends to melodic aspects of music. Melody and rhythm appear to be neurologically dissociated, with the left hemisphere apparently better at processing the latter. The right hemisphere also provides and interprets the melodic nuances of speech, the tone of voice, which is important for conveying affective or emotional connotations of speech. Melody has emotional content for both music and language (Wallin, et al., eds., 2000: 203–204).

Table 1-5. Schematic of the left and right hemispheres

Left hemisphere	Right hemisphere
Analytical processing	Global/holistic processing
Right hand, right visual field	Left hand, left visual field
Language	Visuospatial skills, recognise faces, Melody
Rhythm	
Time sequencing	Emotions, tone of voice, humour, metaphor

(Wallin, et al., eds., 2000: 205)

According to Koelsch (2012: 242), both music and speech require decoding of acoustic information. With regard to acoustics, the term timbre and phoneme are equivalent, because both are characterised by amplitude and spectrum, the two physical correlates of timbre. The identification of timbres in music is paralleled by the identification of phonemes in language.

However, the segmentation of phonemic information during language perception usually requires a higher temporal resolution compared to music perception, because timbral information in music does not change as rapidly as phonemic information in language. This leads to left hemispheric weighting for the segmentation of phonemes during language perception, whereas segmentation of spectral information, such as melodic information of speech prosody or musical melodies, engages the right auditory cortex more strongly than the left auditory cortex. This functional hemispheric specialisation of the auditory cortex can be observed already at birth.

Recent auditory experimental evidence has shown that extensive plasticity is possible in adulthood. Adults can hear or discriminate various sounds. Nevertheless, it does appear that neural circuitry emerging during development can constrain the plasticity seen later in life, especially in the field of musical perception (Rees & Palmer, eds., 2010: Chapters 15 & 16).

Table 1-6. Hypothesised organisation of musical and linguistic structures

Exclusively musical	Shared structures	Exclusively linguistic
Fixed pitches, scales, intervals	Durational patterns	Word meaning, parts of speech
Harmony	Grouping	Truth conditions, reference, entailment
Counterpoint	Stress	Grammatical units
Tonality	Metrical grids	Phonological distinctive features
Pitch prolongations	Contour	Phonological structures

(Arbib, ed., 2013: 272)

Patel (2008), systematically emphasising commonalities over differences, claims that music and language share a number of basic processing mechanisms although having specialised representations, such as pitch intervals in music and nouns and verbs in language. These mechanisms include the ability to form learned sound categories, to extract statistical regularities from rhythmic and melodic sequences, to integrate incoming elements, such as musical tones and words into syntactic structures, and to extract nuanced emotional meanings from acoustic signals.

On the surface, music and speech have one very obvious difference in their sound category systems. Pitch is the primary basis for sound categories in music, such as intervals and chords, while timbre is the primary basis sound for categories of speech, such as vowels and consonants. However, Patel (2008: Chapter 2) reveals that there is growing evidence that music and speech share mechanisms for sound category learning even though the two domains build their primary sound categories from different features of sound. Although the end products of sound category learning in music and speech are quite different, the processes that create sound categories have an important degree of overlap.

Music and speech involve the systematic temporal, accentual and phrasal patterning of sound. Both are rhythmic. One similarity is grouping structure. Elements such as tones and words are grouped into higher level units, including phrases. A key difference is temporal periodicity, which is widespread in musical rhythm but lacking in speech rhythm. Linguistic rhythm is the product of a variety of interacting phonological phenomena and not an organising principle unlike the case of music. Furthermore, empirical comparisons of musical and spoken melody are a recent endeavour. Despite important differences between the melodic systems of the two domains, there are numerous points of contact between musical and linguistic melody in terms of structure and processing. Neuropsychological research indicates that melodic contours in music and speech may be processed in an overlapping way in the brain (Patel, 2008: Chapters 4 & 5).

1.3. Sounds of human language

One of the fundamental questions of language is how listeners map the acoustic signals onto syllables, words and sentences, resulting in understanding of spoken language. In the listener's first language, this mapping is fast and effortless, taking place so automatically that in everyday conversation we rarely think about how it might occur. Studies of speech signals have provided much evidence that the system contains a great deal of underlying complexity that is not evident to the casual listener (Hillis, ed., 2015: Chapter 13).

When listening to speech, the first requirement is that the continuous speech sound is perceptually segmented into discrete entities, such as features, segments, and syllables, that can be mapped onto and will activate abstract phonological representations that are stored in long-term memory. The incoming and unfolding acoustic input activates not only one but a whole set of lexical candidates in parallel. This set of candidates is reduced to the one that fits best based on further incoming acoustic input and contextually based predictions. This word recognition process is completed extremely fast within a few hundred milliseconds (Arbib, ed., 2013: Chapter 9).

The study of linguistic sound systems is divided into phonetics and phonology. Phonetics is the science of speech sounds, and includes the study of the acoustic structure of speech and the mechanisms by which speech is produced and perceived. Phonology is the study of the sound patterns of language, and includes the study of how speech sounds are organised into higher level units, such as syllables and words, how sounds vary as a function of contest, and how knowledge of the sound patterns of language is represented in the mind of a speaker or listener (Patel, 2008: 37).

1.3.1. Human hearing system

The human auditory system is capable of transforming

a continuous acoustic signal into neural representations that provide access to word meaning information. Whilst exactly how this is accomplished has yet to be fully determined, recent technological advances have greatly enhanced the understanding of this complex phenomenon (Hillis, ed., 2015: Chapter 14).

The crucial aspect of coding of amplitude and frequency is that different places in the cochlea are tuned to different frequencies. This tuning is known as the place code for sound frequency: tuning of different parts of the cochlea to different frequencies, in which information about the particular frequency of an incoming sound wave is coded by the place along the cochlear partition that has the greatest mechanical displacement (Wolfe, et al., 2012: 254).

As we can distinguish different visual objects, the hearing system is able to discriminate different sounds. This holds not only for single sounds, such as the successive tones of a melody or the successive vowels and consonants of a word, but even for simultaneous sounds, such as those produced by multiple musical instruments in a concert or the mix of voices at a cocktail party. The most striking property of the hearing system is its ability to analyse the world of superimposed sounds and to separate them according to their various sources.

Despite the appearance of effortlessness in ordinary conversation, three basic characteristics of speech complicate the decoding task of a listener (Vihman, 2014: 51):

1. **Speech flows**

    Although pauses occur at the end of sentences, clauses, and phrases, stretches of spontaneous speech of five to ten words are often produced without interruption. The lack of any reliable overt marking of boundaries is one aspect of the segmentation problem.

2. **Speech sounds vary**

    Every aspect of speech production is subject to multiple sources of variation. There is no direct proportional relationship between the vocal tracts of men, women, and children. The formant frequencies that define the vowel space differ from speaker to speaker in complex ways. Even for a single speaker, rate of speech and loudness of delivery each exert significant effects on the signal. This can be interpreted as follows: humans can process the same musical note played by different instruments as we have seen before, and

this mechanism is employed to perceive /i/ sounds spoken by men, women and children.
3. **Articulatory gestures interact**
   As a result of the dynamic nature of speech production, the same identifiable phonetic segments will be expressed by different acoustic patterns even within a single utterance, depending on their position in the word or syllable and on the immediate phonetic context. Coarticulation refers to the overlapping of articulatory movements associated with two or more phonetic segments.

Each individual sound consists of several frequency components. The ear distinguishes between frequency components originating from different sound sources, as opposed to components from the same source. The harmonics of a tone are not heard individually but fuse into a single percept with features of pitch, loudness, and timbre.

Speech perception does not depend on the extraction of a simple invariant acoustic pattern directly available in the speech waveform. This has been illustrated both by perceptual studies and by attempts to build machines that recognise speech. A given speech sound is not represented by a fixed acoustic pattern in the speech wave; instead, the speech sound's acoustic pattern varies in a complex manner according to the preceding and following sounds.

Speech is intelligible at a rate of 400 words per minute, which corresponds to a rate of about ten phonemes per second. Because the articulators take time to move between the locations required for different phonemes, the shape of the vocal tract is changing almost continuously. In free-flowing speech, a vowel sound is not a static pattern of spectral peaks but is constantly changing as the articulators in the vocal tract move between the position corresponding to one speech sound and the position corresponding to the next speech sound. This is called coarticulation, which implies that the sound waveform corresponding to a particular phoneme is heavily modified by the nature of the phonemes before and after (Plack, 2014: 200).

One of the earliest findings cited as support for the existence of a specialised processing mode for sound perception was categorised perception in which continuous stimuli is perceived in a categorical fashion. Liberman presented listeners with stimuli from a synthetically generated continuum of stop consonants that varied in place of articulation from /b/ to /d/ to /g/. In addition, listeners are faced with substantial variation in the speech signal, yet they are able to recover the speaker's intended utterance automatically without conscious awareness.

Speech is a multidimensional stimulus varying in a complex way in both frequency and time. The ability to handle speech variability declines with age. Older listeners are affected more by talker and amplitude variability than young listeners.

Part of a word that is highly probable in the context of a sentence may be heard even when the actual acoustic cues for that part are minimal or absent. This kind of filling-in process often occurs when listening in noisy environments.

Visual information contributes to speech intelligibility. Listeners are able to correctly perceive more words in noise when visual information is available, as listeners integrate information from the two sensory modalities in order to recover the intended utterance. About 30% of speech can be understood accurately with the addition of visual information (lip reading) in English (Ball, et al., eds, 2008: Chapter 24). Some people prefer to look at the speaker's face during a lecture or a speech so that they can see the movements of the speaker's mouth. In cartoons and music videos, it is more natural and comfortable to see the shapes of the mouth that articulate the heard sounds than those that do not match them.

Individual differences in the shape of the vocal tract will affect the spectrum of the vowel. The most obvious differences are between men, women, and children. For instance, the frequencies of the first three formants in the /i/ phoneme are around 340, 2300, and 3000 Hz in men; 430, 2800, and 3300 Hz in women; and 450, 3100, and 3700 Hz in children. More data can be found in Chapter 2. The vocal tract characteristics for individual men, women, and children vary, and the way speech sounds are produced varies depending on the particular accent of the speaker.

The huge variability of speech has important consequences for the auditory mechanisms that interpret this information. Recent experimental studies have shown that our brains do not search for the characteristics of individual phonemes in the speech waveform but process sounds over a longer period of time, recognising the temporal transitions that are associated with coarticulation and even calibrating for the individual speaker's voice characteristics (Plack, 2014:

209). Speech perception is associated with the dorsolateral temporal lobes. This is largely because speech is an acoustic signal, and the dorsolateral temporal lobes contain auditory cortical fields.

To achieve a description consistent with the known functioning of the auditory system, the dimensions of intensity, frequency, and time must be shown simultaneously. A display of this type is the spectrogram, which shows how the short-term spectrum of speech usually plotted on a linear frequency scale varies with time (Moore, 2013: Chapter 9).

Speech spectrographs are a very convenient means of displaying the acoustic characteristics of speech in a compact form. Frequency, time, and amplitude can be analysed in a spectrographic display. A spectrograph analyses a speech wave into its frequency components and shows variation in the frequency components of a sound as a function of time. This allows us to see more detail regarding the articulation of the sounds.

On a spectrogram, time is represented by the horizontal axis and given in milliseconds. The vertical axis represents the frequency, which is the acoustic characteristic expressed in cycles per second (Hz). The amplitude is marked by the darkness of the bands. The greater the intensity of the sound energy present at a given time and frequency, the darker will be the mark at the corresponding point on the screen.

Table 1-7. Sound properties analysed by spectrograph

Frequency	• Frequency relates to the individual pulsations produced by the vocal cord vibrations for a unit of time. The rate of vibration depends on the length, thickness, and tension of the cords, and is different for the speech of children, adult males and adult females.
	• A speech sound contains two types of frequencies. The first, fundamental frequency, relates to vocal cord function and reflects the rate of vocal cord vibration during phonation. The other formant frequency relates to vocal tract configuration.
Time	Time as a property of speech sounds reflects the duration of a given sound.
Amplitude; intensity	The amplitude of a sound refers to the amount of subglottal air pressure.

(Yavaş, 2006: 97)

Individual differences in sound perception relate to the wide range of aspects, including the processing sounds in native and foreign languages. The following components of auditory perception were proposed based on scientific investigations (Barclay, 2012: 13; Harley, et al., 1997: Chapter 9):

1. **Awareness of sound**
   Auditory awareness is noted by the ability to change behaviour by the presence of sound. Voices or environmental sounds are sounds that even infants will react to almost from birth.
2. **Auditory attending**
   Auditory attending is the intention to listen or accept responsibility for processing language or nonlanguage sound stimuli. The person who is auditory attending not only is aware of the sound but also tunes in the sound. This is the ability to focus on a single source of auditory information.
3. **Auditory attention span**
   Auditory attention span is the span that a person can attend selectively to language or nonlanguage sounds. If the learner is motivated, the learner's attention span over a period of time with auditory perception can be increased. Maintenance of records with the use of good auditory materials at the learner's level should

help to increase auditory attention span.

4. **Sound localisation**

   Localisation of sound requires the location of the direction from which a language or nonlanguage sound originated. Reaching to an object by sound alone was found to occur much later than reaching for object by sight.

5. **Auditory discrimination**

   Auditory discrimination is the ability to recognise and respond appropriately to similarities and differences in language or nonlanguage sounds. Auditory discrimination tests measure the ability to hear accurately the differences that exist between the phonemes. The learner is asked to listen to pairs of sounds that are the same word or differ by only one phoneme and to indicate similarity or difference.

6. **Auditory memory**

   Auditory memory is the ability to store and recall auditory material, such as a sound or series of language or nonlangauge sounds. If the learner cannot remember certain sounds, it would be difficult to associate an object with the sound or to interpret the meaning of the sound.

7. **Auditory memory span**

   Auditory memory span refers to an individual's ability to remember the nature or characteristics of a sound over an increasing length of time. Auditory memory span applies to the remembering of words. The number of words recalled in word and reading span tests predicts comprehension of learners.

8. **Auditory sequencing ability**

   The ability to remember the order of items in a sequence of language or nonlangauge sounds is called auditory sequencing ability. An example of such sequencing occurs when the learner recalls 'John goes' after 'John goes to the store' is spoken.

9. **Auditory projection ability**

   Auditory projection is defined as the ability of the learner to attend to and interpret language or nonlangauge sounds that come from a distance. Some people are only able to attend to and process sounds that are in the immediate vicinity. This issue is as described the broadcasting voice. Some learners need help to listen at increasingly greater distances.

10. **Auditory figure ground discrimination**

    Auditory separation is comparable to the visual

skill of figure ground discrimination. It is the learner's ability to attend to a particular sound or series of sounds when other competing sounds are also present. It is like listening to a teacher's instruction while a radio or television set is playing in the same room. The listener must ignore distracting background noises in order to pay attention to a particular sound selectively.

11. **Auditory blending**

    Auditory blending is the ability to blend speech sounds. It is sometimes described as the ability to synthesise isolated phonemic sounds into a whole word.

12. **Auditory closure**

    Auditory closure is the ability to identify the true or accurate pronunciation of a word. It is sometimes described as the ability to synthesise some of the separate sounds of a word into a whole word, sometimes called auditory interaction. An auditory closure test consists of having the learner supply a completed word from an incomplete stimulus word, e.g., daddy from day.

13. **Re-auditorisation**

    Re-auditorisation is the unvoiced recollection and holding of a sound production. This recollection is important in speech development. If infants imitate an inflection pattern heard from their mothers, they must remember and hold for reference for future reproduction the sound characteristics of the signal.

1.3.2. Listening to a foreign language

It is much harder to listen to and understand speech in a foreign language than in the first language. The efficiency of processing our first language rests in the adaptation of speech processing to the phonological structure of the mother tongue.

Listening in a foreign language draws on the same architecture as listening in the first language, but the adaptation to the first language means that this efficient auditory system is maladapted to differently structured input from another language. The most important factor in perception of foreign language phonemes is the mapping between the phonemic repertoires of the two languages. The thirteen aspects of audition in Section 1.3.1 have an influence on speech learning.

Putting them in another way, Cutler (2012: Chapter 9) lists the following requirements for foreign language listeners to understand the flow of speech:

Table 1-8. Difficulties in foreign language sound processing

Distinguishing minimal interword contrasts: A problem arises when the phoneme contrasts required by a foreign language differ to a greater or lesser degree from the contrasts that distinguish the words of the first language.
Activating words from memory: The listener's foreign language vocabulary is much smaller than that in the first language, and the foreign language words that are known will have been heard less often.
Segmenting continuous speech into its component words: The sequence constraints and boundary-related probabilities that work well for the first language are not exactly the same as those in a foreign language.
Constructing sentences from the resulting words: Prosodic, syntactic, and semantic relations pose problems in understanding the flow of speech.

Speech learning requires the ability to establish central perceptual representations for a range of physically different phonemes that signal differences in meaning, and the development of motoric routines for outputting sounds in speech production (James &

Leather, eds., 1997: Chapter 1; for more empirical studies, see Nakamori, 2009: Chapters 3–5).

Speech perception is highly constrained by phonemic categories of the first language, but this does not mean that the perceptual system has lost the sensitivity required to distinguish contrasts in a foreign language. Various studies have revealed that perceptual sensitivity is sufficient to discriminate the contrasts, but in the early stage of learning when the learner lacks enough input, the highly established categorisation processes of the first language tend to exclude acoustic distinctions that are not relevant to the first language. This phenomenon is called perceptual assimilation or perceptual magnet.

The ability to perceive phonemes in a foreign language does not necessarily mean that this ability will be correctly deployed to discriminate words, and the inability to perceive a contrast does not necessarily rule out accurate encoding of the contrast in lexical entries. For instance, it has been shown frequently that Japanese learners of English confuse /l/ and /r/ sounds, but from the listener's point of view, listening is never consciously about perceiving phonemic contrasts, but it is about understanding messages. No one says that Japanese people sometimes eat lice in the morning. However, as we will see in Chapter 3, they would need to practise how to articulate these sounds correctly; otherwise, these errors are somewhat troublesome in communication.

The difficulty of listening to continuous speech cannot be simply predicted from success in phonemic discrimination. This is because segmentation of speech involves its own procedures. All languages modify complicated sequences in connected speech in order to simplify the articulation process, but the manner in which this is done varies from one language to another. Most native speakers are totally unaware of such a simplification process.

Segmentation draws on listeners' knowledge of the language-specific probalistic patterns of word-boundary occurrence. If segmentation processes appropriate for a foreign language do not match the phonology of the first language, listening to the foreign language becomes much harder. Stress, rhythm and intonation (prosody) are the main issues in foreign language segmentation. As we will discuss in Chapter 7, phonological chunking strategies are required to decode meanings accurately from the sequences of sounds at natural speed.

Prosodic effects span more than one individual

speech segment. Basically, Japanese does not have word stress variation, having all syllables equally stressed within the word. Every syllable is spaced equidistantly in time, called mora timing. On the other hand, English has word stress variation, having its stressed syllables delivered on an equally spaced basis, with unstressed syllables being fitted within the dominant regular arrival of primary stressed syllables. This results in drastic sound changes, deletion, and weak forms, all of which are peculiar to English.

In natural speech, the vowels and consonants that we hear as separate units are not in fact separate at all. The vocal tract is in continual motion without any pauses between segments. During the production of speech, any particular articulator is required to go through a rapid sequence of varied gestures. The position that an articulator achieves for a sound is likely to be influenced by the position during the previous sound, and the position it will be required to move towards for the following sound (Ashby & Maidment, 2005: Chapter 8).

1.3.3. Flexibility and plasticity in the auditory system

Everyday experience makes it seem that hearing or

auditory processing requires little if any effort under normal circumstances. However, extensive research indicates that understanding information presented through the auditory channel can place significant demands on the attentional resources, particularly in challenging listening environments or when multi-tasking is required (Hoffman, et al., eds., 2015: Chapter 16).

The auditory modality has several unique characteristics that result in specific advantages and disadvantages. One main advantage of audition is that it does not require the listener to be in any particular location. Sound can be used to present information to someone who is moving around, distracted, or visually/tactually engaged in another task. On the other hand, although several early experiments pointed to a speed and accuracy benefit for signals presented in the auditory modality, subsequent research has called into question the generality of this advantage and noted that when stimulus intensity is carefully controlled, auditory performance advantages generally disappear.

Listeners are confronted by several problems when understanding foreign language speech. Firstly, language is spoken at about ten phonemes per second, so it requires rapid processing. It is said that we can understand speech speeded up to 5–6 sounds or phonemes per second in our mother tongue. Secondly, there is a segmentation problem, which is difficulty in separating out or distinguishing words from the pattern of speech sounds. Thirdly, there is coarticulation in normal speech, which is the overlapping of adjacent articulations. Fourthly, there are significant individual differences from one speaker to the next. In addition, listeners in everyday life have to contend with degraded speech. Some people are talking at the same time or there are distracting sounds (Eysenck & Keane, 2010: 355–356).

In perception, the inflexibility of the human language processing system with respect to nonnative phonology contrasts most strikingly with the extreme flexibility we can demonstrate within our own language. We can cope effortlessly with different speakers and different listening conditions. Previously unheard voices may be immediately understood; speech from men's, women's and children's vocal tracts is equally comprehensible despite the enormous acoustic variation caused by differences in vocal tract size; we can comprehend speech in spite of background noises, radical band pass restriction, as in telephone conversations, or vocal tract obstruction, such as a cold in the nose or a mouthful of food. However, the robustness of our native language perception often does not carry over to other languages (Otake & Cutler, eds., 1996: 1).

Many middle-aged and elderly people claim that they are bad at listening to foreign languages and accented speech. It is apparent that a number of anatomical, molecular genetic, and chemical changes in the aging central auditory system play roles in functional declines in sound processing with age. Many changes at lower levels of the auditory pathway, such as the cochlear nucleus, are driven by age-dependent cochlear deafferentation, whereas some changes at higher levels of the system can occur somewhat independently of peripheral changes, such as the noteworthy decline in the auditory efferent feedback system that occurs in middle age.

However, in the last twenty years, evidence from human studies has revealed that the adult auditory system exhibits a remarkable degree of plasticity. Such plasticity has been demonstrated using a wide range of experimental paradigms in which auditory input or the behavioural significance of particular inputs is manipulated. A type of learning/practice that is characteristic of all perceptual systems, termed perceptual learning, improves discriminative ability. This provides further evidence that adult sensory systems are modifiable by experience (Rees & Palmer, eds., 2010: Chapters 16 & 17).

Native language listeners excel in adapting rapidly to newly encountered talkers, dialectal variation, unfamiliar accents, new words and language change. Listener adaptability rests on the inherent plasticity of categorical decisions in speech perception. The boundaries of native language phonemic categories are not immutably fixed but can be adjusted as the listening situation requires. Category decisions are adjusted to take account of sequence constraints, phonetic context, rate of speech and higher level probabilities. They are also adjusted to deal with individual pronunciation idiosyncrasies. Perceptual learning is speaker specific and long-lasting and it generalises beyond the learning situation to facilitate continued communication. Early acquired languages command an advantage over later learned languages simply because of the rich amount of constant exposure and experiences (Cutler, 2012: Chapter 11).

Chapter 2

Description of English sounds and learning problems

Introduction

The Japanese language has a fairly simple sound system compared to English. Japanese consists of twenty-six distinct consonants and five vowels, whilst English has a much more complex sound system, consisting of twenty-four consonants and twenty vowels with some dialectal variations (Hasegawa, 2015: Chapter 3).

In the following sections, we will have a close look at vowels and consonants of English. The descriptions and acoustic data are quoted from Ball & Müller (2005) with permission from the authors. Professor Ball acknowledged that most of the acoustic data in the formant tables for vowels, etc. were quoted by them from Alan Cruttenden's book. I would regard Cruttenden (2008) as the ultimate source for the formant tables.

2.1. Vowels

One major binary division of speech sounds is into the categories of vowels and consonants. A strictly phonetic definition of the difference between these two classes of sounds would be that consonants involve contact or near contact between the relevant articulators, whereas vowels do not; that is to say, there is a wide gap between the articulators.

With consonants, it is relatively straightforward to adopt the articulatory approach as we do in Section 2.2, because the articulators are usually fairly to very close together and we can use our own sense of touch and movement to work out their relative positions and their movements during sound production. On the other hand, vowels are somewhat more difficult to describe from an articulatory viewpoint, because there is no contact or near contact between the articulators, and it is difficult for us to sense exactly where they are and how they move. We need to know the tongue shape (convex or concave), tongue height on the vertical axis within the vowel area (high, half-high, half-low, or low), and tongue position on the horizontal axis (front, central or back). Since vowels are produced in a comparatively large part of the oral cavity, even very slight movements of the tongue or the lips can produce different vowel qualities (Ball & Müller, 2005: Chapter 5).

Vowels are complex tones with characteristic spectra. The relative levels of the harmonics depend on the vowel sound that is being produced. The waveforms and spectra of vowel sounds consist of a series of harmonics and there are peaks in the spectra called formants. Different vowel sounds are characterised by the frequencies of the various formants. Formants correspond to resonances in the vocal tract, which behaves like a pipe that is open at one end. The size and shape of the cavities in the mouth and throat determine the resonant frequencies that will be present, and these properties are affected by the positions of the articulators, especially the tongue. The spectrum of the vowel sound or the identity of the vowel sound depends on the positions of the articulators (Plack, 2014: 197). Vowels are highly resonant, demonstrating at least two formant areas. Vowels are more intense than consonants, so they are typically louder than consonants.

Vowels are characterised by distinct patterns of

vocal tract resonances, the formants. Research has shown that the formants of a particular vowel are not all equal in terms of how much they contribute to the listener's perception of that vowel. When formants are close in frequency, the listener integrates the two into one perceptual unit, which is the equivalent of the average of the two closely spaced formants. While there is no strict one-to-one correspondence between vowels and their formant frequencies, this blurring of the boundaries between vowels is not usually a problem for listeners. Individuals are able to compensate for the differences or similarities in formant frequencies within and between vowels.

Note that listeners with hearing impairment often show impaired frequency resolution. This lack of ability to discriminate between frequencies might be expected to interfere with perception of vowels, which depends to a large degree on the ability to detect subtle differences in formant frequencies. Many individuals with high-frequency losses confuse vowels such as /i/ and /u/. The F1 of these sounds are fairly close in frequency, and the F2 for /i/ is relatively high in frequency, which may not be detected by hearing-impaired people.

Although there are far fewer studies that have

investigated for vowel errors than consonant errors, there are a number of good reasons for targeting vowel errors as a part of a speech training programme for first and foreign languages, such as to improve intelligibility, increase speech acceptability, accelerate progress, and restore normal developmental or learning patterns. However, any approach requiring learners to focus on their own articulatory activity may be somewhat more difficult with vowels than with consonants. The high degree of vocal tract constriction involved in consonant production generally results in high levels of tactile feedback, which enhance awareness of articulatory placement. With the exception of close vowels, this tactile feedback is generally decreased during vowel production. There are six common approaches available, each focusing on one of the following: auditory perceptual skills; linguistic abilities; motor skills; the development of perceptual or phoneme awareness skills; the visual feedback of acoustic information; and the visual feedback of articulatory information (Ball & Gibbon, eds., 2013: Chapter 17).

The production of vowel errors may be associated with auditory perceptual difficulties. Auditory input approach emphasises the importance of learners listening to native speakers producing well-formed utterances containing target sounds. According to this position, the training does not require learners to produce target sounds. This position holds that it is not necessary to include production practice, because the increased opportunities to hear target speech sounds are sufficient to induce positive changes in output. This is true in the mother tongue and first language environment, but is not guaranteed in foreign language environments with limited and accented input. This approach maximises auditory salience of target speech sounds by placing them in contexts that involve maximally clear productions. This approach presupposes that perception and production mechanisms are closely related, and perception controls production unconsciously.

Linguistic approaches emphasise the importance of contrasts and communicating meaning and integral components of the learning process. Well-known examples are minimal pair contrast and maximal oppositions. Learners are encouraged to listen to and repeat these pairs in words and sentences.

Training to develop motor or articulatory skills follows the general principles of motor learning, which emphasise the importance of providing repetitive, intensive and systematic drills. These drills are used to establish consistency in articulation and reduce variable performance. Motor approaches also emphasise the significance of knowledge of results in the form of verbal, visual, tactile and kinaesthetic feedback on performance.

Computers offer new possibilities for engaging learners in auditory discrimination and identification tasks nowadays. I have conducted a series of studies investigating a procedure with speech analysis software in the Japanese foreign language learning context (Nakamori, 2009: Chapter 5). The use of computer-assisted visual feedback derives its effectiveness from making ambiguous internal cues explicit, and enabling conscious control of such cues to develop. Through real-time feedback, the speaker has the opportunity to monitor and change the behaviours of the tongue and other articulators using techniques that provide feedback using visual displays.

Visual feedback about tongue position can be achieved using techniques such as glossometry, electropalatography and ultrasound. Physiological techniques can provide feedback about articulatory features, such as tongue height and its relative position in the front or back dimension, all of which are crucial for vowels. With these technologies, accurate measurement for medical treatment is provided, but in classroom settings, it would be less handy and difficult to adopt them at present.

The following sections summarise the main characteristics of English vowels.

2.1.1. High front tense vowel

A high front tense unrounded vowel, /i/, can occur word-initially, before and after consonants, and word-finally in open syllables. The highest point of the tongue arch is raised to a position slightly behind and below the highest, frontest position possible for a vowel.

The side rims of the tongue may make light contact with the inner surfaces of the upper side teeth. The tongue is tense during the production of this vowel, which belongs to the group of long vowels. The lip shape for the vowel is spread.

Table 2-1. Typical formant values for /i/

	F0	F1	F2	F3
Men	138	342	2322	3000
Women	227	437	2761	3372
Children	246	452	3081	3702

2.1.2. High front lax vowel

A high front lax unrounded vowel, /ɪ/, can occur word-initially, before and after consonants, but not word-finally in open syllables. This phoneme is produced with the highest point of the tongue arch raised to a position substantially behind and below the highest, frontest position possible for a vowel.

The side rims of the tongue may make light contact with the inner surfaces of the upper side teeth. The tongue is lax during the production of this vowel, which belongs to the group of short vowels. The lip shape of the vowel is slightly spread.

Table 2-2. Typical formant values for /ɪ/

	F0	F1	F2	F3
Men	135	427	2034	2684
Women	224	483	2365	3053
Children	241	571	2552	3403

2.1.3. Mid front lax vowel

A mid front lax unrounded vowel, /ɛ/ or /e/, can occur word-initially, before and after consonants, but not word-finally in open syllables. This phoneme is produced by raising the highest point of the tongue arch to a position about halfway between the highest, frontest position possible for a vowel and the low front position.

The side rims of the tongue may make light contact with the inner surface of the upper side teeth. The tongue is lax during the production of this vowel, which belongs to the group of short vowels, but not as lax as for /ɪ/. The lip shape for this vowel is loosely spread.

Table 2-3. Typical formant values for /ɛ/

	F0	F1	F2	F3
Men	127	580	1799	2605
Women	214	731	2058	2979
Children	230	749	2267	3310

2.1.4. Low front lax vowel

A low front lax unrounded vowel, /æ/, can occur word-initially, before and after consonants, but not word-finally in open syllables. The highest position of the tongue arch is lowered to the lowest position possible for a vowel.

The rear side of the tongue may make light contact with the inner surfaces of the upper side teeth. The tongue is lax during the production of this vowel, which belongs to the group of short vowels, although it is noticeably longer than other lax vowels but tenser than /ɪ/ or /ɛ/. The lip shape for the vowel is neutrally open.

Table 2-4. Typical formant values for /æ/

	F0	F1	F2	F3
Men	123	588	1952	2601
Women	215	669	2349	2972
Children	228	717	2501	3289

2.1.5. Low back tense vowel

A low back tense unrounded vowel, /ɑ/, can occur word-initially, before and after consonants, and word-finally in open syllables. The highest point of the tongue arch is lowered to a position slightly in front of the lowest, backest position possible for a vowel to make this phoneme.

The side rims of the tongue make no contact with the inner surfaces of the upper side teeth. The tongue is tense during the production of this vowel, which belongs to the group of long vowels. The lip shape for the vowel is neutrally open.

Table 2-5. Typical formant values for /ɑ/

	F0	F1	F2	F3
Men	123	768	1333	2522
Women	215	936	1551	2815
Children	229	1002	1688	2950

2.1.6. Mid back vowel

A half-low back rounded vowel, /ɔ/, can occur word-initially, before and after consonants, and word-finally in open syllables. The highest point of the tongue arch is raised to a position about a quarter of the way up from the lowest, backest position possible for a vowel.

The side rims of the tongue make no contact with the inner surfaces of the upper side teeth. The tongue is more tense than lax during the production of this vowel, which belongs to the group of long vowels. The lip shape for the vowel is open rounded.

Table 2-6. Typical formant values for /ɔ/

	F0	F1	F2	F3
Men	121	652	997	2538
Women	210	781	1136	2824
Children	225	803	1210	2982

2.1.7. Low back rounded vowel

A low back rounded vowel, /ɒ/, can occur word-initially, before and after consonants, but not word-finally in open syllables. This is a lax vowel. The highest point of the tongue arch is lowered to a position close to the lowest, backest position possible for a vowel.

The side rims of the tongue make no contact with the inner surfaces of the upper side teeth. The tongue is lax during the production of this vowel, which belongs to the group of short vowels. The lip shape for the vowel is open rounded.

Table 2-7. Typical formant values for /ɒ/

	F1	F2
Men	593	866
Women	602	994

2.1.8. High back lax vowel

A high back lax vowel, /ʊ/, cannot occur word-initially, but can before and after consonants, although not word-finally in open syllables. The highest point of the tongue arch is positioned substantially in front of and below the highest, frontest position possible for a vowel to produce the most frequently occurring phoneme.

The side rims of the tongue make no contact with the inner surfaces of the upper side teeth. The tongue is lax during the production of this vowel, which belongs to the group of short vowels. The lip shape for the vowel is closely and loosely rounded.

Table 2-8. Typical formant values for /ʊ/

	F0	F1	F2	F3
Men	133	469	1122	2434
Women	230	519	1225	2827
Children	243	568	1490	3072

2.1.9. High back tense vowel

A high back tense rounded vowel, /u/, can occur word-initially, before and after consonants, and word-finally in open syllables. The highest point of the tongue arch is raised to a position slightly in front of and below the highest, backest position possible for a vowel.

The side rims of the tongue make no contact with the inner surfaces of the upper side teeth. The tongue is tense during the production of this vowel, which belongs to the group of long vowels. The lip shape for the vowel is close rounded.

Table 2-9. Typical formant values for /u/

	F0	F1	F2	F3
Men	143	300	997	2343
Women	235	459	1105	2735
Children	249	494	1345	2988

2.1.10. Low nonrhotic central vowel

A half-low unrounded central vowel, /ʌ/, can occur word-initially, before and after consonants, but not word-finally in open syllables. This phoneme is produced by raising the highest point of the tongue arch to a position centrally between front and back, and a quarter of the way from the lowest to the highest position.

The side rims of the tongue make no contact with the inner surfaces of the upper side teeth. The tongue is somewhat tenser than for schwa during the production of this vowel, which belongs to the group of short vowels. The lip shape for the vowel is neutrally open.

Table 2-10. Typical formant values for /ʌ/

	F0	F1	F2	F3
Men	133	623	1200	2550
Women	218	753	1426	2933
Children	236	749	1546	3145

2.1.11. Mid nonrhotic lax central vowel

A mid unrounded central vowel, /ə/, can occur word-initially, before and after consonants, and word-finally in open syllables. The highest point of the tongue arch is positioned centrally between front and back, and midway from the lowest to the highest position, i.e. virtually in the centre of the vowel area.

The side rims of the tongue make no contact with the inner surfaces of the upper side teeth. The tongue is lax during the production of this vowel, which belongs to the group of short vowels. The lip shape for the vowel is neutrally open.

Table 2-11. Typical formant values for /ə/

	F1	F2
Men	478	1436
Women	606	1695

2.1.12. Front mid-closing diphthong

This diphthong, /eɪ/, is a glide from a mid front tongue position toward a higher, backer position similar to that of /ɪ/. This phoneme has the highest point of the tongue arch raised to a fully front position halfway between the lowest and the highest positions. The tongue glides from here upward toward the position of

/ɪ/, this glide being accompanied by slight closing of the jaw.

The side rims of the tongue make light contact with the inner surfaces of the upper side teeth. As with all the English diphthongs, the tongue is tense during the production of this vowel, which belongs to the group of long vowels. The lip shape for the vowel is spread.

Table 2-12. Typical formant values for /eɪ/

	F1 initial	F2 initial	F1 final	F2 final
Men	587	1945	413	2130
Women	581	2241	416	2204

2.1.13. Central mid-closing diphthong

This diphthong, /əʊ/, is a glide from a mid central tongue position toward a higher, backer position similar to that of /ʊ/. The highest point of the tongue arch is raised to a central position halfway between the lowest and the highest positions to produce this phoneme. The tongue glides from the position upward and backward toward the position of /ʊ/, this glide being accompanied by a slight closing of the jaw.

The side rims of the tongue make no contact with the inner surfaces of the upper side teeth. The lip shape for the vowel is neutral at the start, changing to open rounded.

Table 2-13. Typical formant values for /əʊ/

	F1 initial	F2 initial	F1 final	F2 final
Men	537	1266	379	1024
Women	545	1573	380	1267

2.1.14. Front low-closing diphthong

This diphthong, /aɪ/, is a glide from a low front tongue position towards a higher position similar to that of /ɪ/. The highest point of the tongue arch is placed at a fully low position somewhat retracted from the frontest possible one. The tongue glides from there almost directly upward toward the position of /ɪ/, this glide being accompanied by a considerable closing of the jaw. In rapid speech, the tongue glide may not always reach the /ɪ/ position.

The side rims of the tongue make light contact with the inner surfaces of the upper side teeth toward the end of the glide. The lip shape for the vowel starts neutrally open and ends loosely spread.

Table 2-14. Typical formant values for /aɪ/

	F1 initial	F2 initial	F1 final	F2 final
Men	734	1117	439	2058
Women	822	1275	359	2591

2.1.15. Back low-closing diphthong

This diphthong, /aʊ/, is a low nearly central tongue position toward a higher, backer position similar to that of /ʊ/. This phoneme is produced by placing the highest point of the tongue arch at a fully low position retracted from the frontest possible one to a near central one. The tongue glides from this position upward and backward toward the position of /ʊ/, this glide being accompanied by a considerable closing of the jaw. In rapid speech, the tongue glide may not always reach the /ʊ/ position.

The side rims of the tongue make no contact with the inner surface of the upper side teeth during the glide. The lip shape for the vowel starts neutrally open and ends loosely rounded.

Table 2-15. Typical formant values for /aʊ/

	F1 initial	F2 initial	F1 final	F2 final
Men	780	1368	372	1074
Women	901	1538	403	1088

2.1.16. Fronting low-closing diphthong

This diphthong, /ɔɪ/, is a glide from a mid-low back tongue position toward a higher, fronter position similar to that of /ɪ/. The highest point of the tongue arch is set at a mid-low back position. The tongue glides from there upward and forward toward the position of /ɪ/, this glide being accompanied by a considerable closing of the jaw. In rapid speech, the tongue glide may not always reach the /ɪ/ position.

The side rims of the tongue make light contact with the inner surfaces of the upper side teeth toward the end of the glide. The lip shape for the vowel starts open rounded and ends loosely spread.

Table 2-16. Typical formant values for /ɔɪ/

	F1 initial	F2 initial	F1 final	F2 final
Men	477	824	443	1924
Women	428	879	334	2520

2.1.17. High front centring diphthong

This diphthong, /ɪə/, is a glide from a tongue position similar to that of /ɪ/ toward a mid central position. The highest point of the tongue arch is set at the position of /ɪ/. The tongue glides from there toward and backward toward a mid central position, this glide being accompanied by a slight opening of the jaw. In rapid speech, the tongue glide may not always reach the absolute mid central position.

The side rims of the tongue make light contact with the inner surfaces of the upper side teeth at the start of the glide. The lip shape for the vowel starts loosely spread and ends in a neutral shape.

Table 2-17. Typical formant values for /ɪə/

	F1 initial	F2 initial	F1 final	F2 final
Men	382	2096	578	1643
Women	399	2514	417	1846

2.1.18. Mid front centring diphthong

This diphthong, /ɛə/, is a glide from a mid front tongue position similar to that of /ɛ/ toward a mid central position. The highest point of the tongue arch is set at the position of /ɛ/. The tongue glides from this position upward and backward toward a mid central position, this glide being accompanied by very slight closing of the jaw. In rapid speech, the tongue glide may not always reach the absolute mid central position.

The side rims of the tongue make light contact with the inner surfaces of the upper side teeth at the start of the glide. The lip shape for the vowel remains neutral throughout.

Table 2-18. Typical formant values for /ɛə/

	F1 initial	F2 initial	F1 final	F2 final
Men	538	1864	655	1594
Women	691	2210	751	1883

2.1.19. High back centring diphthong

This diphthong, /ʊə/, is a glide from a high back tongue position similar to that of /ʊ/ toward a mid central position. It can occur before and after consonants and word-finally in open syllables but not initially. The highest position of the tongue arch is set at the position of /ʊ/.

The tongue glides from there downward and forward toward a mid central position, this glide being accompanied by very slight opening of the jaw. In rapid speech, the tongue glide may not always reach the absolute mid central position. The lips for the vowel start loosely rounded and finish in a central shape.

Table 2-19. Typical formant values for /ʊə/

	F1 initial	F2 initial	F1 final	F2 final
Men	426	1028	587	1250
Women	420	1157	485	1258

2.2. Consonants

Consonants are associated with restrictions in the flow of air through the vocal tract, caused by a narrowing or closure of a part of the vocal tract.

Consonants can be categorised in terms of the manner of the constriction that occurs: how the sounds are formed. The airflow is directed or altered to produce different classes of sound.

Plosives or **stop** consonants are produced with a complete constriction, a total interruption in the flow of air. In other words, there is a blocking of the airflow followed by an abrupt release, which results in an explosive sound. They are made when two articulators contact each other and momentarily block the flow of air through the oral cavity. Just behind the blockage, oral air pressure builds up and is then released explosively when the blockage is released. The burst of air that is released as the stop sound.

Fricatives are caused by very narrow constrictions,

leading to a noisy burst of sound. The articulators come very close together at some point in the oral cavity so that air is forced at speed through a small space, resulting in audible friction. These sounds occur when air is forced through a narrow channel somewhere within the oral cavity under high pressure. The narrow channel is formed when two articulators come close to each other but do not touch.

Affricates are produced when complete blocking of the airflow, as in the plosives, is followed by release through a narrow space, like in the fricatives. They are made by combining features of stops and fricatives. The sound begins its life as a stop, but changes in midstream to end up as a fricative.

Approximants are produced by partial constrictions. The articulators approach contact but are not so close that friction is produced. These sounds are usually produced with vibration of the vocal folds. The name **glide** suggests a smooth flowing movement, and this indeed describes how these sounds are produced, with the tongue shifting smoothly and rapidly from its position for one vowel to a position for another vowel. The glide sound emerges during this shift. **Liquids** have the property of flowing, so the name of this category of sounds suggests that airflow through the oral cavity is smooth and flowing. The tongue forms a loose blockage within the oral cavity, allowing air to flow around the blockage and out the mouth.

Nasals are produced by preventing airflow from the mouth and allowing air to flow into the nasal passages by lowering the soft palate. Air is released through the nasal cavity. The soft palate is lowered to allow the air to escape through the nose. For all other sounds, the soft palate is raised to prevent nasal escape of air.

Consonants are categorised in terms of the place at which the constriction occurs: the position in the mouth where the articulators make contact or move close together.

Causing a complete constriction at the lips produces **bilabial** sounds. These sounds involve the lips as the articulators.

The tongue tip is in contact with the upper teeth to produce **dental** sounds. A narrow constriction between the tongue and the teeth produces dental fricatives.

The bottom lip is in contact with the upper teeth to make **labiodental** sounds.

Alveolar sounds are produced when the tongue tip

is in contact with or close to the alveolar ridge, on the roof of the mouth, which is behind the upper teeth.

Palatoalveolar sounds are made when the blade or middle of the tongue is in contact with or close to the region just behind the alveolar ridge.

If the blade of the tongue is in contact with or close to the hard palate, **palatal** sounds are produced.

Velar sounds are produced if the back of the tongue contacts or is close to the soft palate.

A **glottal stop** is produced when the vocal folds close to block the airflow from the lungs, and then abruptly come apart to release the flow of air.

Finally, consonants are categorised into voiced or unvoiced, depending on whether the vocal folds are vibrating around the time of constriction (Lancaster, 2008: Chapter 2; Plack, 2014: 198).

Table 2-20. Acoustic correlates of consonantal features

Voiced	vertical striations corresponding to the vibrations of the vocal folds
Bilabial	locus of both second and third formants comparatively low
Alveolar	locus of second formant about 1700-1800 Hz
Velar	usually high locus of the second formant; common origin of second and third formant transitions
Retroflex	general lowering of the third and fourth formants
Plosive	gap in pattern, followed by burst of noise for voiceless stops or sharp beginning of formant structure for voiced stops
Fricative	random noise pattern, especially in higher frequency regions, but dependent on the place of articulation
Nasal	formant structure similar to that of vowels but with nasal formants at about 250, 2500 and 3250Hz
Lateral	formant structure similar to that of vowels but with formants in the neighbourhood of 250, 1200 and 2400 Hz; the higher formants considerably reduced in intensity
Approximant	formant structure similar to that in vowels, usually changing

(Ladefoged & Johnson, 2015: 214)

Table 2-21. The consonants of English

	Nasals	Plosives	Fricatives	Affricates	Approximants (glides & liquids)
Bilabial	m	p, b			w (glide)
Labiodental			f, v		
Dental			θ, ð		
Alveolar	n	t, d	s, z		ɹ, l (liquids)
Palatoalveolar			ʃ, ʒ	tʃ, dʒ	
Palatal					j (glide)
Velar	ŋ	k, g			
Glottal		ʔ	h		

In the flowing sections, we summarise the characteristics of each consonant sound of English and then focus on the common consonant errors in pronunciation by native and Japanese speakers of English. All of the speech errors that native speakers and other foreign language learners can possibly make are not included.

2.2.1. Plosive sounds

Plosives all consist of the three stages of stop production: a shutting phase, where the articulators come together to produce an air-tight seal somewhere in the oral cavity; a closure phase lasting some 40 – 150 milliseconds, where the air from the lungs is stopped in the mouth, resulting in a build-up of air pressure behind the closure; and the release phase, when the articulators part and the compressed air rushes out with a popping noise. It is essential that the aspiration of voiceless /p,t,k/ in accented positions be maintained as the major factor distinguishing these phonemes from voiced /b,d,g/, i.e. aspiration constituting a more potent differentiating feature than the presence or absence of voicing.

Bilabial plosives: /p/ /b/

For /p/, the vocal folds are abducted (held apart) in the voiceless phonation posture throughout the sound. The upper and lower lips are brought together, mainly through a closing movement of the lower jaw, and an air-tight seal is formed between them. Air from the lungs is pressurised behind this closure, which lasts for around 100–140 milliseconds. At the end of this period, the lips are parted mainly through movement of the lower jaw, and the compressed air rushes out with a popping noise. After the release of the articulators, some time will pass (about 60 milliseconds) before vocal fold vibration commences the following segment, resulting in aspiration. Throughout the articulation, the tongue is likely to be moving into position for the following segment.

For /b/, the vocal folds are vibrating in the voiced phonation posture throughout all or most of the sound. The upper and lower lips are brought together, mainly through a closing movement of the lower jaw, and an air-tight seal is formed between them. Air from the lungs is pressurised behind this closure, which lasts for around 60 milliseconds. At the end of this period, the lips are parted mainly through movement of the lower jaw, and the compressed air rushes out with a popping noise. Throughout the articulation, the tongue is likely to be moving into position for the following segment.

Alveolar plosives: /t/ /d/

To produce /t/, the vocal folds are abducted in the voiceless phonation posture throughout the sound. The tongue tip and/or blade is raised until it touches the alveolar ridge, and an air-tight seal is formed between the tongue and the alveolar ridge, and between the side rims of the tongue and inner surface of the upper side teeth. Air from the lungs is pressurised behind this closure, which lasts for around 100 – 140 milliseconds. At the end of this period, the tongue lowers, and the compressed air rushes out with a popping noise. After the release of the articulators, some time will pass (about 65 milliseconds) before vocal fold vibration commences for the following segment, resulting in aspiration. Throughout the articulation, the lip shape is likely to be influenced by the following segment.

The /d/ sound is made with the tongue tip and/or blade raised until it touches the alveolar ridge, and an air-tight seal is formed between the tongue and the alveolar ridge and between the side rims of the tongue and inner surface of the upper side teeth. The vocal folds are vibrating in the voiced phonation posture throughout all or most of the sound. Air from the lungs is pressurised behind the closure, which lasts for around 50 – 60 milliseconds. At the end of this period, the tongue lowers and the compressed air rushes out with a popping noise. Throughout the articulation, the lip shape is likely to be influenced by the following segment.

Velar plosives: /k/ /g/

For /k/, the vocal folds are abducted in the voiceless posture throughout the sound. The back of the tongue dorsum is raised up until it touches the soft palate, and an air-tight seal is formed between the tongue and the velum. Air from the lungs is pressurised behind this closure, which lasts for around 100 – 140 milliseconds. At the end of this period, the tongue dorsum is lowered, and the compressed air rushes out with a popping noise. After the release of the articulators, some time will pass (about 60 milliseconds) before vocal fold vibration commences for the following segment, resulting in aspiration. Throughout the articulation, the lip shape will be under the influence of the following sound.

For /g/, the vocal folds are vibrating in the voiced phonation posture throughout all or most of the sound. The back of the tongue dorsum is raised up until it touches the soft palate, and an air-tight seal is formed between the tongue and the velum. Air from the lungs is pressurised behind this closure, which lasts for around 60 milliseconds. At the end of this period, the tongue dorsum is lowered, and the compressed air rushes out with a popping noise. Throughout the articulation, the lip shape will be under the influence of the following sound.

2.2.2. Fricative and affricate sounds

Fricatives are sounds made by air being forced through a narrow gap and are commonly replaced by plosives where air is built up and suddenly released explosively.

Labiodental fricatives: /f/ /v/
The vocal folds are abducted in the voiceless phonation posture throughout the sound. The inner surface of the upper lip is brought into close approximation with the undersurface of the upper front teeth, mainly through a closing movement of the lower jaw, and a narrow channel is left between them. Air from the lungs flows through this channel and becomes turbulent. Throughout the articulation, the tongue is likely to be moving into position for the flowing segment.

For /v/, the inner surface of the upper lip is brought into close approximation with the undersurface of the upper front teeth, mainly through a closing movement of the lower jaw, and a narrow channel is left between them. Air from the lungs flows through this channel and becomes turbulent. The vocal folds are vibrating in the voiced phonation posture throughout all or most of the sound. Throughout the articulation, the tongue is likely to be moving into position for the following segment.

Dental fricatives: /θ/ /ð/

For /θ/, the vocal folds are abducted in the voiceless phonation posture throughout the sound. The tongue tip is raised to make a close approximation behind the upper front teeth or between the upper and lower front teeth, and a narrow channel is left between them. The channel has a wide slit shape. Air from the lungs flows through this channel and becomes turbulent. Throughout the articulation, the lip shape will be influenced by the following segment.

For /ð/, the vocal folds are vibrating in the voiced phonation posture through all or most of the sound. The tongue tip is raised to make a close approximation behind the upper front teeth or between the upper and lower front teeth, and a narrow channel is left between them. The channel has a wide slit shape. Air from the lungs flows through this channel and becomes turbulent. Throughout the articulation, the lip shape will be influenced by the following segment.

Alveolar fricatives: /s/ /z/

The sound /s/ is produced with the vocal folds abducted in the voiceless phonation posture and with the tongue tip and/or blade raised up to make a close approximation with the alveolar ridge; a narrow channel is left between them. The channel has a narrow grooved shape. Air from the lungs flows through this channel and becomes turbulent. Throughout the articulation, the lip shape will be influenced by the following segment.

For /z/, the vocal folds are vibrating in the voiced phonation posture through all or most of the sound. The tongue tip and/or blade is raised up to make a close approximation with the alveolar ridge, and a narrow channel is left between them. The channel has a narrow grooved shape. Air from the lungs flows through this channel and becomes turbulent. Throughout the articulation, the lip shape will be influenced by the following segment.

Postalveolar fricatives: /ʃ/ /ʒ/

The vocal folds are abducted in the voiceless phonation posture throughout the production of /ʃ/. The tongue blade is raised to make a close approximation to the rear of the alveolar ridge, and a narrow channel is left between them, which has a narrow slit shape. At the same time, the front of the tongue body is raised toward the front of the hard palate. Air from the lungs flows through this channel and becomes turbulent. Throughout the articulation, the lip shape will be influenced by the following segment, although many speakers use a rounded lip shape in almost all contexts.

When producing /ʒ/, the vocal folds are vibrating in the voiced phonation posture through all or most of the sound. The tongue blade is raised to make a close approximation to the rear of the alveolar ridge, and a narrow channel is left between them. The channel has a narrow slit shape. At the same time, the front of the tongue body is raised up toward the front of the hard palate. Air from the lungs flows through this channel and becomes turbulent. Throughout the articulation, the lip shape will be influenced by the following segment, although many speakers use a rounded lip shape in almost all contexts.

Glottal fricative: /h/

This sound is produced with the vocal folds abducted. Air from the lungs is forced through the glottis under pressure and becomes turbulent. Throughout the articulation, the position of the articulators in the oral cavity will be influenced by the following segment, so the sound quality of /h/ depends on what vowel follows it.

Postalveolar affricates: /tʃ/ /dʒ/

The vocal folds are abducted in the voiceless phonation posture throughout the sound. The tongue tip and blade are raised up until they touch the rear part of the alveolar ridge, and an air-tight seal is formed between the tongue and the alveolar ridge and between the side rims of the tongue and the inner surface of the upper side teeth. At the same time, the front of the tongue is raised toward the hard palate, leaving only a narrow channel. Air from the lungs is pressurised behind this closure, which last for about 100 milliseconds. At the end of this period, the tongue tip and blade lower slightly, and the compressed air is forced through the narrow channel left between the front of the tongue and the hard palate and between the blade of the tongue and the alveolar ridge. The channel has a narrow slit shape. The durations of the stop part and the fricative part are roughly equal. Throughout the articulation, the lip shape is likely to be influenced by the following segment, although many speakers normally use a rounded lip shape for this sound.

To make the voiced version of this sound, the tongue tip and blade are raised until they touch the rear part of the alveolar ridge, and an air-tight seal is formed between the tongue and the alveolar ridge and between the side rims of the tongue and inner surface of the upper side teeth. At the same time, the front of the tongue is raised toward the hard palate, leaving only a narrow channel. Air from the lungs is pressurised behind the closure, which lasts for around 40 milliseconds. At the end of this period, the tongue tip and blade lower slightly, and the compressed air is forced through the narrow channel left between the front of the tongue and the hard palate and the blade of the tongue and the alveolar ridge. The channel has a narrow slit shape. The vocal folds are vibrating in the voiced phonation posture throughout all or most of the sound. The durations of the stop part and the fricative part are roughly equal. Throughout the articulation, the lip shape is likely to be influenced by the following segment, although many speakers usually use a rounded lip shape for this sound.

Table 2-22. Examples of error patterns of fricatives

Target word	Child's pronunciation	Japanese learners
fair, leaf	pair, leap	where, whee-who
van, cave	ban, cabe	ban, cabe
thumb, Ruth	tum, root	fum/some, roof/roose
these	gede	dedz, dese, geez
sun, peace	ton, Pete	sun, peace
zip, maze	dip, made	gip, madz
shoe, mash	two, mat	shoe, mash
chin, match	tin, mat	chin, match
jam, badge	Dam, bad	dzam, bach

The fricatives and affricates are a large group of sounds in English, and they develop between the ages of two and a half and seven years. The sounds f and s are usually the first to develop, and are present in the speech of children aged two and a half to three years. The sh sound emerges more slowly and will often sound more like s until children are four or five years old. It is not unusual for the voiceless th to sound like f, and voiced th to be pronounced as v or d, even until a child is aged seven. In some dialects of English, there is no th sound, so thin sounds like fin or tin, and there sounds like vair or dair in adult speakers. The affricates might be produced in simplified forms until the age of five. As these sounds develop, children might produce them as fricatives, where chair sounds like shair and jam like zham (the zh is the sound in measure), or they might front the affricates, so chair sounds like tsair and jam sounds like dzam.

2.2.3. Gliding

This section focuses on the problems with the approximants l and r. The sounds l and r are produced as the earlier developing sounds y and w.

Alveolar lateral approximant: /l/

There are two distinct variants of /l/ produced in English. These two main variants differ in their articulation. The first main variant is given the name clear-l and the second is termed dark-l.

Clear-l is produced in the following way. The vocal folds are vibrating in the voiced phonation posture throughout all or most of the sound. The tongue tip and/or blade is raised up until it touches the alveolar ridge, and the side rims of the tongue are lowered so that the air flows over the side of the tongue. There may also be a certain amount of raising of the front of the tongue toward the hard palate. The channel shape for the airflow is wide enough so that the air remains laminar without friction. Whereas some speakers have air flowing over both sides of the tongue, others have unilateral airflow; there appears to be no perceptible sound difference between these states. Throughout the articulation, the lip shape is likely to be influenced by the following segment.

Dark-l is produced as follows. The vocal folds are vibrating in the voiced phonation posture throughout all or most of the sound. The tongue tip and/or blade is raised up until it touches the alveolar ridge, and the side rims of the tongue are lowered so that the air flows over the side of the tongue. The channel shape for the airflow is wide enough that the air remains laminar without friction. At the same time, the back of the tongue dorsum is raised up toward the soft palate, though without touching it. Some speakers have air flowing over both sides of the tongue, whereas others have unilateral airflow. Some speakers tend to use a rounded lip shape with dark-l, whereas for others rounding only results if the preceding vowel is rounded. The dark-l sound is found in syllable-final position after vowels and before consonants.

Postalveolar central approximant: /ɹ/

There are two distinct ways of producing approximant-r. While the two forms both sound the same, the tongue position differs. The first category is a postalveolar approximant (apical-r or retroflex-r) and the other variety is termed a bunched-r.

Apical-r is produced in the following way. The vocal folds are vibrating in the voiced phonation posture throughout all or most of the sound. The tongue tip is curled up toward, but not touching, the alveolar ridge, and the front of the tongue is lowered. The back of the tongue is somewhat higher than the front, so there is a hollow in the body of the tongue. Air flows centrally over the tongue without turbulence. Throughout the articulation, the lip shape is likely to be influenced by the following segment, although many speakers use lip rounding always for this sound, or always unless the following vowel is spread. Some speakers may bend the tongue tip back as well as raising it, to produce retroflex rather than a postalveolar articulation.

The vocal folds are vibrating in the voiced phonation posture throughout all or most of the sound to reduce the bunched-r. The tongue dorsum is raised up toward the boundary between the hard and soft palate, and the tongue tip is drawn back into the body of the tongue. There may be some contact between the side rims of the tongue and the insides of the upper molar teeth, but air is allowed to flow freely over the centre of the tongue without turbulence. Many speakers use lip rounding for this sound in all contexts or except when a following vowel is spread.

Labial velar semivowel approximant: /w/

This sound consists of a double articulation and is produced as follows. The vocal folds are vibrating in the voiced phonation posture throughout all or most of the sound. The two lips are in close approximation and assume a rounded shape with some lip protrusion. The back of the tongue dorsum is raised up toward the soft palate but does not touch it. Air flows centrally over the tongue without turbulence.

Palatal semivowel approximant: /j/

The vocal folds are vibrating in the voiced phonation posture throughout all or most of the sound. The front of the tongue dorsum is raised toward the hard palate but does not touch it. Air flows centrally over the tongue without turbulence. Lip shape is determined by the following sounds.

Table 2-23. Examples of error patterns of gliding

Target word	Child's pronunciation	Japanese learners
light	yight, white	right, white
leg	yeg, weg	reg, weg
road	woad, yoard	woad
rain	wain, yain	wain

Difficulties with these sounds are very familiar in children's speech, and some adults continue to mispronounce r. The l sound is usually acquired by age three and a half, but is sometimes still produced as a y in the word yellow, pronounced as yeyow until beyond this age. The r is a late developing sound and is usually accurately produced by age six.

2.2.4. Context sensitive voicing

The consonants that are usually voiceless at the beginning of words and syllables are produced as voiced, and those usually produced as voiced at the end of words and syllables are voiceless. This pattern can affect sounds other than the stops p, t, and k.

Table 2-24. Examples of error patterns of voicing

Initial consonant		Final consonant	
Target word	Child's pronunciation	Target word	Child's pronunciation
pen	ben	web	wep
ten	den	bid	bit
coat	goat	beg	beck

Typically developing children usually have a voicing contrast by the age of three. This pattern does tend to persist in children with delayed speech development and is referred to as stopping and fronting where it might combine with these other patterns.

2.2.5. Approximant cluster reduction

The focus is on learners to produce an approximant when it is preceded by another consonant in a word. There are many of these combinations in English: claw, crash, flat, free, glow, grease, play, and pram.

In speech production, the term cluster refers to two or more consonants that occur in sequence within a syllable. The sequence is b, c/k, f, g or p followed by l, r or w. Learners who demonstrate approximant cluster reduction miss one of these consonants in the sequence.

Table 2-25. Examples of error patterns of approximant cluster reduction

Target word	Pattern 1	Pattern 2
pram	pam, bam	ram, wam
play	pay, bay	lay, jay
brick	bick	rick, wick
blue	boo	loo, you
crash	cash, gash	rash, wash
claw	caw, gore	law, your
grease	geese	reese, weese
glow	go	low, yo
free	fee, vee	ree, wee
flag	fag, vag	lag, yag

Most children produce approximant clusters by the time they are four years old. The clusters may not be completely accurate until the child is five and a half or six years. Thus, flag might sound like fyag, crash might sound like cwash, and brick more like bwick. In typical development, children sometimes go through a phase of saying the clusters but with a vowel between them: play – puhlay, brown – burown, green – gureen, and floor – fuhloor.

2.2.6. s cluster reduction

The focus is on helping learners to produce s when it

is followed by other consonants at the beginning of a word, such as in the words sweep, stone and scream, and at the end of a word, such as in the words desk, wasp and post. Learners who demonstrate s cluster reduction miss one of these consonants in the sequence sl, sk, sm, sn, sp, st and sw.

Most four-year-olds are beginning to get the hang of s clusters, especially at the end of words, but they are usually among the more difficult classes of sound sequences to master, and children may not say them all correctly, particularly those with three consonants, like spl and spr, until they are five years old.

Table 2-26. Examples of error patterns of s cluster reduction

Target word	Pattern 1	Pattern 2
smack	mack	sack
snail	nail	sail
spin, crisp	pin/bin, crip	sin, cris
store, mast	tore/door, mart	sore, mas
skip, desk	kip/gip, deck	sip, des
slow	low	sow
sweet	weet	seat

In the group of s clusters where the s is followed by a plosive, such as spin, stare and skate, the written form of the word is a bit misleading. The written form implies a voiceless plosive. When these plosives are preceded by s, they are closer to the voiced sounds. To pronounce as voiceless sounds, learners tend to insert vowels after s. From a speech point of view, the words would be more accurately written as sbin, sdate and sgate.

Chapter 3

Production of speech: articulatory control

Introduction

It has been said, "Every time you say a word, you perform a miracle". Yet those of us who use words so freely and so easily take them for granted, forgetting that oral communication probably is the most important and most complex of all human behaviours (Curtis, 1987: 1).

The principal vehicle for conveying meanings, thoughts, ideas, concepts and attitudes through sounds is articulation. Articulation is the adjustments and movements of speech structures and vocal tract necessary for modifying the breath stream for producing the phonemes and prosodic features of speech. Articulation is the mastery of phonological rules and contrastive features that govern the perception and production of speech. The readily distinguishable speech mechanism adjustments that produce different speech sounds include the following: how intelligible the speaker is; how well the speaker's speech meets the cultural standards; how appropriate the speech is; and how satisfied the speaker is with the speech.

This chapter focuses on how people produce speech sounds and the way to attain fluent articulatory control of a foreign language. Starting from voice control to vowel and consonant articulation, we will look closely at the articulatory training for speech.

3.1. Voice function

Speech production is marked by rapid, coordinated movements of the vocal articulators. This is an impressive feat given the large number of muscles involved in producing even the simplest monosyllable. Fluent speakers meet these demands with relative ease, producing as many as four to seven syllables per second (Goldrick, Ferreira & Miozzo, eds., 2014: Chapter 28).

Speaking is a highly complex motor act, and involves extensive areas in the premotor and motor cortex, the supplementary motor area, and the basal ganglia and cerebellum. Motor cortex activation is associated with the direct control of individual muscles of articulation, while the premotor and supplementary motor areas are important in coordination of muscle groups and in more complex aspects of speech control.

In the 2000's, research in this area showed tremendous progress due to more advanced understanding of the complexities of brain functions related to speech production. For instance, Maassen (2010) presented recent and theoretical developments of research on speech motor control.

The ability to speak depends on a steady outflow of air that is vibrated by the vocal folds to produce a basic sound, which is then further modified by the articulators to generate the specific speech sounds of whatever language is being spoken. Without this outflow of air, there would be no speech.

3.1.1. Voice production

Let us first look at the mechanism of voice production. The voice producing system consists of three basic components: the respiratory system that provides an excess pressure of air in the lungs (respiration); the vocal folds that chop the air stream from the lungs into a sequence of quasi-periodic air pulses (phonation); and the vocal tract that gives each sound its characteristic final spectral shape and thus its timbral identity (articulation) (Deutsch, ed., 2013: 70).

If an individual is simply breathing and not talking, the vocal folds lie relaxed and open to allow free passage of air. A series of muscles in and around the larynx pulls the vocal folds taut when speech is required. The degree of stress on the folds dictates the tone of voice.

When speech is produced, air is pushed from the lungs into the throat by the diaphragm. Then the vocal folds, which reside toward the top of the throat, vibrate in response to the airflow from the lungs and under muscle control, and finally the vibratory vocal fold waveform causes the vocal tract to resonate. The vocal tract consists of many articulators, such as the tongue, palate, lips, velum, and nasal cavity, that move or are used in different ways to form the sounds of speech due to the articulators changing the shape of the vocal tract and hence its resonance properties.

The vocal folds vibrate at a somewhat periodic rate, with a frequency called the fundamental frequency, ranging from about 80 Hz for males and 320 Hz for children. The pitch of a voice is determined by the fundamental frequency. Men have the lowest pitched voices (about 120 Hz), women produce higher pitches (about 220 Hz), and children produce the highest pitches. The size of a person and hormones affect the rate at which the vocal folds can open and close, such that the bigger the person, the more likely it is that the vocal folds are massive relative to those of a smaller person, and vibrate more slowly, producing a lower pitch.

3.1.2. Voice and individuals

The vocal tract is responsible for the sounds of speech. The basic speech sound is the phoneme. The articulators of the vocal tract change in the manner in which they are used and in the location in which they are placed to produce the phonemes. Different vocal tract shapes, based on the different manner and place of articulation, which lead to the different phonemes of speech, produce different frequencies. Each phoneme has a characteristic frequency called formants.

A spectrograph plots frequency as a function of time, with the level of each frequency component indicated by the darkness of the plot, where dark areas represent more intense levels than light or white areas (Yost, 2006: 216-218).

Table 3-1. Voice and its characteristics

Physical characteristics	Psychological characteristics	Social characteristics
Age	Arousal (relaxed, hurried)	Education
Appearance (height, weight, attractiveness)	Competence	Occupation
Dental/oral/nasal status	Emotional status or mood	Regional origin
Health status, fatigue	Intelligence	Role in conversational setting
Identity	Personality	Social status
Intoxication	Psychiatric status	
Race, ethnicity	Stress	
Sex, sexual orientation	Truthfulness	
Smoker or non-smoker	Familiarity	

Liberman (1996: 47) highly values spectrograms, and hypothesised that spectrograms of speech could become as intelligible to the eye as the sounds are to the ear. His book provides thorough investigations on how to read spectrograms accurately and properly. His team enabled the blind to hear print as a practical consequence. Screen readers for computers or scan and read-out machines are widely used by blind people nowadays.

Whenever we speak, our voices convey information about us as individuals. Table 3-1 summarises some of the kinds of judgements that listeners make when listening to voices (Kreiman & Sidtis, 2011: 2).

3.2. From perception to production

Traditionally, scientists have described the process of producing and perceiving speech in terms of a feedforward system. A feedforward system is one in which a speech plan is constructed and carried out without paying attention to the results. A speaker's thoughts are converted into linguistic representations, which are organised into vocal tract movements (articulations) that produce orderly one-way acoustic output. A listener can then pick up this acoustic signal through hearing (audition), after which it is perceived by the brain, and then converted into abstract linguistic representations and finally meaning.

Producing speech, however, is not strictly that linear and unidirectional. When we speak, we are constantly monitoring and adjusting what we are doing as we move along the process. We do this by using our senses to perceive what we are doing. This is called feedback. In this feedback system, control is based on observed results rather than on a predetermined plan (Gick, Wilson & Derrick, 2013: Chapter 1).

Recent scientific brain studies have shown that posterior auditory areas seem to be very important in controlling speech production, and brain regions associated with linguistic information in speech perception and somatosensory processing are supressed during speech production (Bolhuis & Everaert, eds., 2013: Chapter 14). It is possible that the main link between speech perception and production lies in the posterior motor cortex rather than in the motor cortex.

Auditory perception is needed in language acquisition for speech production to develop normally, but this relationship is not bidirectional, as severe speech motor deficits in development do not necessarily compromise speech perception skills. In the course of development, auditory information about one's linguistic environment and the sound of one's voice is needed to develop speech production skills, while speech perception does not require good speech production skills to develop.

Speech perception skills do not necessarily correlate with speech production skills in development, because different auditory networks are involved in the development of speech comprehension and the control of speech production. For instance, there are two types of Japanese learners of English: Some listeners find it difficult to distinguish /l/ and /r/ sounds, but they can accurately pronounce them. Others can discriminate these sounds but are unable to pronounce them properly.

We monitor our speech while it is produced. It is clear from listening to the speech of hearing-impaired people who learned to speak before experiencing hearing loss that monitoring of speech through hearing plays an important role. This auditory feedback is clearly used to monitor our accuracy in the production of prosodic aspects of speech, such as intonation, loudness, tempo, and voice quality, because these are the most obvious disruptions in the speech of postlingually hearing-impaired individuals, especially if their hearing loss occurred sometime previously.

Phonetic disruptions also occur at the level of individual speech sounds with these speakers. Researchers find inaccuracies in the vowel systems, and that precision in the production of many consonants may also deteriorate over time. Auditory feedback is used to monitor the overall accuracy of classes of vowels and consonants by checking whether they sound correct. Without it, the stored neuromuscular patterns will deteriorate over time and cannot be corrected.

In addition, both tactile and kinaesthetic receptors are found throughout the vocal tract. Tactile receptors are responsible for information about touch and pressure, and kinaesthetic ones inform us about the movement and position of vocal organs. The feedback from these receptors helps speakers monitor the accuracy of the movement and placement of the articulators (Ball & Müller, 2005: 22–25).

Vihman (2014: 47) schematised the implicit and explicit sources of phonological knowledge as follows:

Experience patterning by implicit learning in perception

Practice patterns by implicit learning in production

Perceptual-motor link is established (the creation of articulatory filter)

Experience matched to adult or native-speaker norms by implicit learning in perception

Produce words in priming context by implicit retrieval Induce patterns by implicit learning and attach meaning by explicit learning

3.3. Intelligibility of speech signals

Traditionally, findings supporting the Critical Period Hypothesis provide a biological explanation for age-related differences, but recent models propose that interference from the first language contributes most significantly to the difficulty that adults face in trying to master a phonological system of the target language. It has been investigated whether there are common/universal phenomena among different learners of various age groups who have a wide range of first languages. Like the acquisition of absolute pitch discussed in Section 1.2.2, there might be a biological constraint of developing and losing abilities to process some frequency ranges and to judge pitches absolutely, but vowels and consonants of natural language may well be learned.

Speakers differ in intelligibility, and dialect and

accent significantly impact a listener's ability to extract the linguistic contents of speech. Individual differences in talkers' voices (male/female) affect intelligibility. In addition, accented speech is significantly less intelligible than speech produced by talkers from one's own dialect or accent group.

By definition, intelligibility refers to the degree to which the listener understands the sound signal produced by the talker. In contrast, comprehensibility refers to the degree to which the listener understands utterances produced by the talker in a communication context. Comprehensibility reflects the condition where the talker is speaking in a natural communicative context and the listener uses every source of information available to understand the message.

While intelligibility and comprehensibility are both influenced by factors affecting the predictability of the message, the familiarity of the listener, the listener's motivation to understand the talker's message, and the noise level of the environment, comprehensibility is further influenced by a talker's paralinguistic cues, such as facial expression or gestures, supplementary cues, such as the first letter of the word, situational cues, and strategies that the talker and listener use to manage mutual understanding within the context of their ongoing interaction (Damico, Müller & Ball, eds., 2010: Chapter 4).

Common measures of intelligibility can be divided into two broad classes. The first of these involves a forced choice format called feature analytic measurement. This is presumed to allow specification of the underlying reasons in terms of reduced, distorted or lost articulatory contrasts. A second class includes transcription measures, which can take the form of orthographic renderings of a single word or sentences, or phonetic transcriptions of target segments or syllables (Ball, et al., eds., 2008: Chapter 35).

For instance, as we saw in Chapter 2, the Japanese language has a fairly simple sound system compared to English. Japanese consists of twenty-six distinct consonants and five vowels, whilst English has a much more complex sound system, consisting of twenty-four consonants and twenty vowels with some dialectal variations (Hasegawa, 2015: Chapter 3). Japanese learners of English encounter not only segmentally but also suprasegmentally caused problems.

In learning a foreign language, it is necessary to have realistic goals. It is likely that we will have some traces of a foreign accent. A realistic aim is to speak in a way that is clearly intelligible to our listeners and that does not distract, irritate, or confuse them.

Based on experimental studies, Collins & Mees (2013: 215-216) list 'error rankings for English pronunciation' as follows:

Table 3-2. Error categories and intelligibility

Category 1: **Errors leading to potential breakdown of intelligibility**	1. Confusion of crucial phonemic contrasts in vowel system 2. Confusion of fortis/lenis (/f,k,s/ - /v,g,z/) 3. Consonant clusters 4. Crucial consonant contrasts 5. Deletion of /h/ 6. Word stress
Category 2: **Errors that evoke irritation or amusement**	1. Inappropriate /r/ articulations 2. Dental fricative problems 3. Less significant vowel contrasts 4. Incorrect clear/dark /l/ use 5. Lack of weak forms and sound changes
Category 3: **Errors that provoke few such reactions and may even pass unnoticed**	1. Intonation errors 2. Lack of syllabic consonants 3. Compound stress

3.4. Articulatory and phonological treatment

The way speech sounds are used is part of the language subsystem known as phonology. When articulatory errors occur, the individual is using a sound system that is at variance with the adult native speaker system. The speaker's articulatory skills influence the accuracy with which a message is understood as we saw in the previous section.

3.4.1. Necessity for speech learning

Articulation contributes greatly to the intelligibility of a speaker's message, that is, how much of the message is understood. Consequently, a person with unintelligible errors in articulation and/or phonology may have a communicative handicap.

Learners need to be exposed to accurate pronunciation and they are encouraged to continue to pronounce properly all the time. In the mother tongue environment, this is guaranteed, but in foreign language learning environments, teachers' accents influence on learning processes, which needs to be minimised as possible. Learners are advised to use the newly learned behaviour in situations different from those in which it was learned. These processes are commonly called carry-over, which refers to using the correct sound in other settings with other people for the rest of the learner's career/life.

The need for thorough pronunciation practice/treatment is related to social, cultural, ethnic, educational, and occupational aspects of the learner's environment. It is helpful to know the sequential steps (a can-do list) as below:

Table 3-3. Steps for pronunciation learning

1. I know the sound to master.
2. I can tell whether the sound is at the beginning, middle, or end of a word.
3. I can tell whether the sound is said in the new way or old way.
4. I can say the sound in the new way.
5. I can say the sound in the new way in nonsense syllables.
6. I can say the sound in the new way in words.
7. I can say the sound in the new way in sentences.
8. I can say the sound in the new way when I read.
9. I can say the sound in the new way all the time.

(Curtis, 1987: 175)

3.4.2. Sound discrimination and articulatory skills

Much has been investigated on the relationships between sound discrimination and articulatory skills. The rationale for articulatory training for better discrimination is that speech is learned through the ear. A person has to hear a sound several times before all its features are perceived and tuned. On the other hand, the rationale for not using articulatory training is that individuals usually can learn to produce correct sounds without it. In fact, discrimination between correct and incorrect productions is learned during production training when the learner is provided feedback as to the correctness of the sound produced.

It is now widely known that learners who misarticulate a sound have difficulty discriminating their own misarticulations from the correct sound as produced by another speaker, such as their teachers. However, they have no difficulty with the task when comparing their own recorded misarticulations with correct productions. This suggests that learners learn to compare accurately their own errors with correct sound production rather than receiving training in discriminating errors produced by other speakers. Learners should learn pronunciation with their recorded voices. It would not seem to be efficient to spend much time on auditory training with learners who can already discriminate their misarticulation from the correct sound by means of monitoring skills (Curtis, 1987: 182).

As seen in Section 3.2, perception and production are processed differently in our brain even if they are related. This means that rich exposure to the target sounds and ample opportunities to articulate them are required. Many simultaneous interpreters reflect that while they can understand wide varieties of English accents, their own pronunciations are far from native-like. This shows that even if people can discriminate small differences in sounds, they are unable to pronounce them. This is why articulation practice is required, especially in foreign languages.

Creagehead, Newman & Secord (1989: Chapter 9) recommend that auditory discrimination training should be intensive and should precede articulation production training. It should extend over several weeks and perhaps months of training. No production should be insisted upon during this period, though in an informal training situation learners will make spontaneous attempts to produce the target sound because communicative, goal-oriented activities most generally stimulate learners to talk.

There is no easy solution as to when to begin articulation production practice. The learner should not be asked to produce sounds at each succeeding production level, such as phoneme, syllable, word, sentence and conversational utterance, until it has been determined that the appropriate speech sound discrimination for that level can be made easily and rapidly. For instance, widely accepted sensory-perceptual training progresses as follows (Bauman-Waengler, 2012: 265):

Ear training
- Learners develop ability to discriminate between the target sound and other sounds, including the irregular production used.
- Learners are not asked to attempt a production of the target sound but only to judge its distinctness from other sounds.

↓

Identification
- Recognition and discrimination of the sound in isolation when contrasted to other and dissimilar sounds.
- Contrasts should first address sounds that are productionally different. Arrange sounds hierarchically from dissimilar to similar.

↓

Isolation
- Teachers say the sound in word-initial, -medial and -final positions.
- Learners are asked to identify the sound and state in which position the sound occurred.

Stimulation
- Learners are bombarded with variations of the target sound and must identify the sound.
- Variations include louder, softer, longer, shorter and different speakers.

Discrimination
- Error productions of the target sound are presented by the teacher. Error productions should mirror those of the learner.
- Learners are asked to detect the error production and then say why it is wrong.
- Perceptual knowledge of correct and incorrect production features must be taught in previous stages.

As seen above, traditional approaches to sound instruction have four major stages: sensory-perceptual training (ear training); production training (establishment); stabilisation; and carry-over.

The goal of the first stage is to define a standard

for the target sound. The learner is not required to produce the sound, but rather the emphasis is on developing an auditory model that will serve as an internal standard. This helps the learner to become aware of making errors. The learner will use this accurate sound image as a basis to monitor and vary productions.

The second stage usually begins after the learner has learned to identify the acoustic features of the new sound to be learned. The learner can recognise the characteristics of the new sound and make some correct judgements about whether a given production is correct or incorrect. The focus of production training is to evoke and establish a new sound pattern.

When a learner has learned to make the target sound accurately though deliberately, the next task is to stabilise that correct response at the simplest to most complicated level of production.

Finally, the learner must gain the ability to use the new sound in conversation.

It is not unnatural to hear a teacher and a learner complain that the sound does not carry over, because the learner performs well under controlled tasks, like reading aloud, but cannot remember to say the sound correctly in natural conversations. One simple activity to overcome this is giving speech assignments in which learners record and listen to their voice by themselves, checking their speech and writing down errors. It is very important to use the new sound in various types of speaking. The learner must be able to use the new sound in sending messages, in interacting socially, in thinking, and in expressing emotions.

Lastly, the learners must learn to use the proprioceptive sense to monitor their own speech. It is not enough to be able to hear whether a production is correct. The learner must also be able to feel it. Exercises to increase proprioceptive awareness of the correct positions and movements of speech include speaking with earplugs, speaking while wearing earphones that supply a masking noise, whispering, and mouthing. Bauman-Waengler (2012: Chapter 9) has listed possible articulatory errors of native and non-native English speakers and has proposed how to overcome them in detail.

The following approaches of speech training have been shown to be effective (Cummings, ed., 2014: 522).

1. Distributed practice (practise a given number of trials/sessions over a longer period of time) rather than massed practice (practise a given number of

trials/sessions in a small period of time).
2. Random practice (different targets are randomly intermixed) rather than blocked practice (different targets practised in separate, successive blocks).
3. Varied practice (practise targets in different contexts) rather than constant practice (practise targets in same context).
4. High number of trials rather than low number of trials.
5. Knowledge of results (feedback only related to correctness of response) rather than knowledge of performance (feedback related to specific aspects of performance).
6. Low frequency feedback (feedback only after some attempts) rather than high frequency feedback (feedback after every trial).
7. Delayed feedback (feedback provided with a delay) rather than immediate feedback (feedback immediately following attempt).

Recent studies have shown that the crucial factors for improvement are opportunities for language use, the importance of native speaker input, and the necessity for perception-production instruction (Bohn & Munro, eds., 2007). Computer speech training aids are considered a possible way of improving the speech of learners. These technical aids are aimed to compensate for auditory feedback.

Most speech systems are using the acoustic signal from a microphone. The visual feedback in real time is based on spectrograms, oscillograms, and waveform envelopes. These aids provide external control over different motor functions depending on the kind of visual feedback. Visual feedback systems are used as effective tools for the modification of speech attributes and intelligibility. Speech training should be accompanied by the development of phonological knowledge and the presentation of symbolic word meanings (Ziegler & Deger, eds., 1998: Chapter 54). The programme can be easily integrated into the English lessons as a supplementary tool. Spectrographic feedback provides accurate measurement of speech production skills in real time and can support the perception and self-regulation of speech (Nakamori, 2009: Chapter 5).

3.5. Phonological encoding and monitoring

In our mother tongue, we usually speak fluently

without any errors, pauses, repetitions, and so on, but we are disfluent when talking in a foreign language. Speakers first plan their speech (phonological encoding) and then check to see if that speech is in accordance with the plan (self-monitoring).

Phonological encoding begins with the word form. Encoding the word form is divided into two processes: one process retrieves the phonological content of the word and the other retrieves the syllabic structure of the word. There is little doubt that speakers listen to themselves when speaking out loud, and scrutinise what they hear. There is an additional channel that monitors speech before articulation. In conversation, speakers not only talk but they also listen to their interlocutors' speech and they monitor their own speech, feedforward and feedback simultaneously.

In our mother tongue, everything has been processed automatically and implicitly, but in a foreign language, we need to process consciously with explicit monitoring. This is why we need training to speed up the processing processes. Learners need to master each step gradually to lessen the processing load, from words to phrases to sentences.

The ability to detect and correct our own speech errors is facilitated by a self-monitoring system that consists of the following two feedback loops (Kemmerer, 2015: Chapter 6):

1. **The external feedback loop** monitors the auditory signals of self-produced speech. It may be implemented in the posterior two thirds of the superior temporal region bilaterally.
2. **The internal feedback loop** monitors the covert process of generating phonological words. Its neural substrates may overlap those of the external feedback loop.

The process of speech production is schematised as follows (Ball, et al., eds., 2008: Chapter 31):

Stored word forms (segments, metrical frames)
↓ **Phonological encoding**
Syllabified phonological words
↓ **Phonetic encoding**
Gestural scores
↓ **Motor execution**
Speech movements and monitoring

Many brain mechanisms underlie voice production, reflecting the many physical, emotional, cognitive and experiential factors associated with the sound a speaker produces at a given moment. Voice patterns emerge out of interactive processes of phonation, articulation and audition. Auditory feedback of one's own voice and self-monitoring are experienced by all language users. To acquire vocal competence, humans must hear the adult language (native speaker norms) at a certain time in their development and they must hear their own voices producing it. When hearing loss affects adults, slow changes in phonated and articulated speech ensue, suggesting a degree of ongoing self-monitoring is necessary to maintain normal speech (Kreiman & Sidtis, 2011: Chapter 6).

Brain imaging studies suggest that self-monitoring and speech comprehension are served by the same neural structures. The external self-monitoring route involves listening to self-produced speech, whereas the internal self-monitoring route involves evaluating the speech plan. There is an essential distinction between these monitoring channels. Self-repair occurs rather rapidly, demonstrating that speakers use an internal monitoring channel in addition to an external auditory channel.

In speech production, speakers listen to their own overt speech and check whether it contains any discrepancies with intended speech. This implies that the language comprehension system is critically involved in monitoring overt speech. In addition, speakers monitor representations of speech that is not yet articulated through an internal channel.

Many researchers interpret that speech production is strictly serial and feedforward only. According to this position, feedback, i.e. monitoring, takes place just before or after production, which might be included in orderly processes. Self-monitoring employs the speech comprehension system, which is also used in listening to the speech of others. The speech being produced reaches the comprehension system via two different routes: the inner route feeding a covert form of not-yet-articulated speech into the speech comprehension system, and the auditory route feeding overt speech into the ears of the speaker. The external route is relatively unimportant in the detection of lexical errors but important in the detection of phonological errors. The division of labour is under top-down control (selective attention to the internal channel) but also depends on bottom-up influences (access to acoustical and phonetic information (Hartsuiker,

Bastiaanse, Postma & Wijnen, eds., 2005).

There are three components of self-monitoring: trouble detecting; stopping; and repairing components (Goldrick, Ferreira & Miozzo, eds., 2014: Chapter 25). There are eleven monitoring channels that have been proposed. They function automatically and simultaneously in first and foreign language processing.

1. Conceptual loop monitor in the conceptualiser checks whether the preverbal message corresponds with the speaker's intentions
2. Lexical monitor for lemma selection
3. Syntax monitor for grammatical frame generation
4. Node activation monitor before phonological encoding
5. Inner loop monitor for speech comprehension
6. Buffer articulation timing monitor before articulation
7. Efference monitor for efferent commands: the motor planning system produces a copy of the commands to the motor system and sends this to a comparison centre where it can be compared with some internal standard or with motor feedback from the actual movement
8. Proprioception monitor for speech motor

movements: short feedback loops between input and output neurons that provide information about the location and direction of movement of the articulators
9. Taction monitor for speech motor movements: somewhat later tactile feedback
10. Auxiliary loop monitor for entire processing
11. Knowledge or results monitored

In the process of first language acquisition, we have built up this system unconsciously, but we need to establish a rapid processor for a foreign language by means of training under limited input. This is a very hard task we encounter.

Since speakers undergo these monitoring processes constantly, as well as listening to what others are saying and building up their thoughts simultaneously, speaking accurately, fluently, and properly is an extremely hard task. Research on language production lags behind that on language comprehension. What we know so far is to speed up phonological decoding and encoding processes by gradual training. We will come back to this matter in Chapter 7.

Chapter 4

Vision, space representation, and tactile sensation

Introduction

What does it mean to see? According to Marr (2010: 3), "The plain man's answer would be, to know what is where by looking." Vision is the process of discovering from images what is present in the world and where it is. If we are capable of knowing what is where in the world, our brains must be representing this information in all its profusion of colour and form, beauty, motion, and detail. A representation is a formal system for making explicit certain entities or types of information, together with a specification of how the system does this.

Visual perception is of enormous importance in our everyday lives. It allows us to move around freely, to see people with whom we are interacting, to read magazines and books, to admire the wonders of nature, and to watch films and television. It is also important because we depend on visual perception being accurate to ensure our survival. The acquisition and processing of sensory information in order to see, hear, taste or feel objects in the world guides an organism's actions with respect to those objects (Eysenck & Keane, 2010: 33).

This book is about blindness, and we wish to understand what vision is and what if it is absent. Cattaneo & Vecchi (2011) clearly state that sighted individuals are used to define a blind person as someone that cannot see, describing his or her experiences borrowing the lexicon of the sighted. However, blindness is not less; it is "alter." Recent research on imagery, spatial cognition and compensatory mechanisms at the sensorial, cognitive and cortical levels in individuals affected by a complete or profound visual deficit has revealed that other sensory channels, such as audition, touch and olfaction, compensate vision, all of which clearly reflect brain mechanisms of the blind.

4.1. Visual perception

Tens of thousands of times every day we identify or recognise objects in the world around us, and our actions are guided visually. Visual perception includes processing of form, depth, size, colour, texture, and motion. Visual perceptual systems analyse colour, shape, and three-dimensional spatial relations, and are concerned with the visual guidance of bodily motions and recognition of faces. The visual system is very efficiently organised to recognise objects, to pick out the ones that need attention, to decide whether they should be grasped or avoided, to remember them, and to do all of this in a brief moment of time. To accomplish this, different aspects are analysed in different areas of the system and in different clusters or columns within those areas.

Over the past decade or so, scientists have learned a great deal about the neural correlates of conscious and unconscious perception and how the disruption of different brain areas can disrupt specific aspects of visual consciousness. A consistent finding is that the primary visual cortex seems to be important for the ability to perceive any visual feature at all, while higher brain areas may be important for perceiving particular visual features or objects (Baars & Gage, 2013: Chapter 6). The following brief explanations on vision are based on Daw (2012) and Purves & Lotto (2011).

4.1.1. Lightness and brightness

The perceptions of lightness and brightness generated by the overall intensity of light stimuli are thought to be the most fundamental qualities that humans and other animals have evolved to see. The amount of light that an object reflects is called its luminance. However, whether it appears black or white, light grey or dark grey, or yellow or brown, depends on its surroundings, and is known as lightness or brightness. Lightness and brightness provide many intriguing examples of the universal discrepancies that exist between physical measurements of the world and what we perceive.

The perception of the lightness of an object depends on contrast with the immediate surroundings and also with interactions with objects further away. This results in a perception where lightness is closely related to the reflectance of the object, helping us to both recognise objects independent of the overall level of illumination and to recognise what other objects are placed around the primary object. If there is a shadow or a boundary of illumination in the field or other transparent objects floating in front, these are usually seen as such.

The factors that determine the distribution of

power in light spectra, the physical correlate of colour perceptions, are inevitably entangled in light stimuli. To see colour, one needs at least two classes of photoreceptors with different spectral sensitivities. A single class of photoreceptors with the same spectral sensitivity will just signal lightness. Humans have four classes: rods and three classes of cones. One can see colour using rods and the red absorbing cones at the appropriate level of illumination. These cones feed into opponent colour cells in the retina, which are either red opposed by green or yellow opposed by blue.

4.1.2. Distance and depth

In addition to conflating the physical parameters that determine the quality and quantity of light reaching the eye, the parameters that define intervals, angles, and object sizes are inextricably intertwined in retinal images. As a result, the real world sources of image forms, like the sources of luminance and the spectral distribution of light, are inherently uncertain. The perception of distance and depth are, like perceptions of lightness, brightness, colour, and form, determined by neural circuitry that reflects the trial and error experience accumulated during evolution and postnatal development.

There are a number of cues to distance and depth perception. Disparity is the most powerful and well known. The cues can be divided into ocular or physiological cues, depending on the position of the eye and lens; kinetic cues, depending on the movement of the scene or the observer; pictorial cues, employed by painters to represent depth on a two-dimensional surface; and stereopsis, depending on disparity. Our sense of depth in the normal world depends on these various cues working together to give an integrated perception.

4.1.3. Objects, faces and motion

The perception of objects and faces are complicated. We are able to recognise a face in a fraction of a second, distinguishing it from numerous other faces. Experts on birds or plants can do the same in their area of expertise. This is true despite variations in the viewpoint or in light and shadow across the object. It also holds for silhouettes and cartoons of a face. A particular face or object activates a number of cells in every area that has been studied. Scientists now refer to distributed coding of face and object identity.

Any approach to vision must also deal with changing spatial relationships and perceptions of motion elicited by image sequences on the retina. There are two aspects of the perception of motion. One is the perception of an object in relation to other objects around it. The other is the perception of the whole scene moving around us, as we navigate through the world. There are different neurons in different areas, different parts of the same area, to deal with these two aspects. The perception of motion entails a variety of puzzling phenomena, including the anomalous way the physical speeds of objects are seen and the dramatic changes in the apparent direction of a moving object that occur when the context is altered.

Finally, all aspects of vision adapt: brightness, colour, contrast, motion, orientation, depth, and faces. It will adapt to combinations of these attributes and to changes in the coordination of vision and the position of the limbs. The simplest form of visual adaption is light and dark adaptation, which enables the system to respond over a range of ten billion in overall level of illumination, when the difference between a white and a black at any particular level of illumination is only one hundred. Then there are a series of aftereffects, such as the waterfall illusion, where looking at a waterfall for several seconds and then switching one's attention to the bank beside the waterfall makes the bank appear to move upward. There are various visuo-motor adaptations.

4.2. Visual and spatial mental representations

For most cognitive scientists, the distinction between visual and spatial representation processing is related to the neurophysiological works reporting that visual and spatial information is processed in different pathways of the brain. From these studies onward, it became common to distinguish between two cortical pathways, called the what and where systems in the brain. The what pathway is responsible for visual object identification, i.e. for the processing of visual properties of objects, such as shape, texture, and colour. The where pathway is responsible for recognising where objects are in space, spatial awareness, and the guidance of actions in space.

There is no doubt that human vision is a very remarkable perceptual system. Vision is a precise and accurate perceptual modality that allows the sighted to extract very useful information about the structure of shapes and objects, the spatial relations among the parts of objects, and the spatial relations among objects in the environment.

However, vision is not the only perceptual modality that allows human perceivers to extract useful information about objects and shapes. Active haptic explorers are also quite fast at perceiving important information in a wide variety of shapes and objects, such as stimulus extent, orientation, and curvature. The haptic perceptual system provides excellent information about a number of dimensions of raised line shapes and objects, surface texture, hardness and softness, and thermal properties.

Young blind school children perform reasonably well in a series of haptic tasks that require material and texture discrimination, spatial orientation, and object naming. They understand the concept of constancy within a series of haptic stimuli that vary in form, shape, texture, or in more than one dimension.

Ordinary people often assume that blind people are bad at obtaining spatial information. However, visual experience is not necessary for solving spatial problems. Moreover, visual illusions also occur in touch (Millar, 2008: Chapters 7 & 8). Accurate shape and spatial perception depend on making use of spatial reference information. Spatial accuracy in vision and touch depend on the reference cues available in a task.

Congenitally blind individuals, who do not experience visual mental images, should be impaired in reasoning with highly visual materials. Several studies have shown that persons who are blind from birth differ from sighted people in their use of visual images, but are as good as the sighted in the construction of spatial representations. People who are blind from birth are able to envisage spatial arrangements but are unable to envisage visual mental images. Most explanations for these results rely on the distinction between the two different neural pathways associated with the processing of what and where information as mentioned before (Knauff, 2013: 15).

Over the past several years, spatial reasoning has gained renewed prominence among educators, as spatial skills are proving to be not just essential to mathematical understanding but also strong predictors of future success beyond the classroom in fields such as science, technology and engineering. Davis (2015) helps to define the concept of spatial reasoning and provides compelling evidence of the need for a clear focus within early education. We will not discuss this issue in this book.

4.3. Spatial cognition in the blind

Researchers have been interested in special cognition in blind people for theoretical and practical reasons. They are concerned about the issue of whether haptic space is Euclidian and whether special cognition develops in a comparative manner in the absence of vision. For instance, unfamiliar tangible pictures may be difficult to name but matching accuracy is excellent, over 90% correct. While congenitally blind people do not all show the spontaneous use of perspective in their drawings, they are able to understand the conventions involved in perspective depictions (Ballesteros & Heller, eds., 2004).

It is well known that both blind and sighted representations of spatial information appear to be analogue, and both groups are equally effective at retaining gist information. Most blind visuo-spatial deficits are the result of processing differences between the blind and sighted. The blind are equally able to remember spatial patterns when they are engaged in a task that does not require their manipulation or elaboration, but a deficit in capacity results in impaired performance of blind people. An understanding of the rules for converting 3D into 2D is vital for tactile picture comprehension. As some conventions cannot be experienced solely through touch, these rules cannot be fully understood by early blind people and are even difficult for those with previous vision to comprehend in haptic-only conditions.

The generation and use of visuo-spatial mental images have a positive effect on memory performance, even in congenitally blind people. Non-sighted people process these mental representations in a specific format that is partially similar and partially different from that of mental images based on visual experience. The required speed of processing, the level of complexity of the representation, and the selective involvement of passive or active visuo-spatial working memory functions are all factors possibly playing a role in determining capacity. The early blind seem to use their visual cortex in tasks for which it was not intended. The visual cortex can have a non-visual function under certain conditions (Hatwell, et al., 2003: Chapters 3 & 10).

A series of recent behavioural and neuroscience results support the idea that both vision and touch may share the same underlying mental representations. Vision and active touch encode the geometrical structure of objects in the same way for familiar and nonsense objects. A large body of findings from several laboratories examining different types of stimuli, such as shapes, objects, and Braille dots, converge on the idea that visual cortical areas in the extrastriate cortex are active during tactile perception. Engineers have been acting on the assumption that touch can substitute for the absence of vision and developed sensory aids and prosthetic devices for blind people.

In the absence of sight, people learn to sharpen their other senses. This idea of sensory compensation has been controversial, but recent research suggests that touch may benefit when vision is not present. An increase in tactile acuity in the absence of sight was found, and this advantage is maintained in older Braille readers. The lack of vision causes changes in the perceptual experience.

Blind people spend considerable time learning to use their senses of touch and audition for pattern perception and for spatial localisation. There are a number of reports of improved auditory memory, including processing of very rapid speech, in early blind people. Enhancement of auditory acuity related to pitch stimuli in the blind is restricted to basic perceptual skills and such enhancement does not depend on prior musical experience but is due to vision loss (Cattaneo & Vecchi, 2011: Chapter 1).

One approach proposed by Harley et al. (1997: 32) is helpful in that it provides a step-by-step sequence of activities that proceed from very gross tactual awareness to the very fine and precise skill of discrimination and recognition of Braille characters.

1. Awareness of and attention to textures and other characteristics of three-dimensional objects.
2. Discrimination of shapes, sizes, weights and directional characteristics of objects so that three-dimensional objects can be recognised and labelled.
3. Recognition of two-dimensional representations, such as geometric shapes, using a variety of materials.
4. Discrimination and recognition of Braille characters.

Finally, I would like to report on a unique case of a blind painter. Artistic expression is a complex behaviour that engages many aspects of perception, cognition and emotion. Painting and drawing represent a form of visual communication associated with the ability to construct, manipulate and ultimately translate the contents of one's own mental representations.

Inherent to this process is the engagement of mental imagery. Current evidence suggests that in sighted individuals, mental representations are pictorial in nature rather than symbolic or verbal. Visual mental imagery is dependent on recollections of prior visual experience. The lack of any prior visual experience would likely impede upon a person's ability to create the visual mental constructs required for artistic expression.

However, it is possible to generate mental pictures via alternate sensory modalities in the absence of any prior visual experience. Early blind individuals are able to represent and communicate the internal representation of objects in their minds through their drawings (Bacci & Melcher, eds., 2013: Chapter 23).

4.4. Integration of acoustic and optic cues

Sensory and motor systems are interdependent and form the sensorimotor system together. The sensory system receives and transmits environmental stimuli from the peripheral sense receptors to the spinal cord to the brain. There is neural integration at every level of the pathway, reshaping the transmitted information. The result is a complex, constantly changing map of oneself, a body scheme, in relation to one's map of the environment. The body scheme is used to inform the motor system to plan, organise and execute movements via muscles. Sensory feedback from a motor response is used in turn to further enhance the body scheme (Pagliano, 1999: 27).

The last few years have seen a dramatic growth of research addressing the question of how the processing of information in the auditory modality is affected by the simultaneous stimulation of one or more of the other senses, such as vision or touch (Calvert, et al., 2004; Pisoni & Remez, eds., 2005: Chapters 3 & 4; Stein, ed., 2012).

4.4.1. Vision over audition and audio-visual integration

One of the best known examples of the dominance of vision over audition occurs when a conflict is introduced between the spatial origin of auditory and visual stimuli. For instance, we typically perceive the voices of the actors in a film as originating from their lips on the screen even though the sounds are often physically presented from loudspeakers situated elsewhere in the cinema. This illusion, called the ventriloquism effect, shows that people tend to mislocalise sounds toward their apparent visual source.

On the other hand, spatially discrepant sounds normally have very little effect on an observer's visual localisation responses, thus demonstrating that vision tends to dominate our perception whenever audio-visual spatial information conflicts. People pay attention to visual input more than auditory information when both stimuli are given simultaneously. When people hear some noise in the closet or bush, then tend to watch the direction well before they actually find a cockroach or a raccoon moving.

When people talk, visual correlates, such as facial and lip movements, are available to the listener. The effect of visual information on speech perception has been extensively studied in the context of the benefit provided by visual cues for listeners with hearing impairment and for speech perception in noise. More than fifty years ago, it was shown that the intelligibility of speech presented in noisy acoustic conditions was significantly higher when people could see the speaker talking. Visual-based enhancement is also observed for undegraded speech with a semantically complicated content or for foreign-accented speech.

In the laboratory, audio-visual integration is illustrated by the McGurk effect. Listeners presented with an acoustic /ba/ dubbed over a face saying /ga/ tended to report hearing /da/, a syllable whose place of articulation is intermediate between /ba/ and /ga/. The robustness and automaticity of the effect suggest that the acoustic and visual articulatory cues of speech are integrated at an early stage of processing (Reisberg, ed., 2013: 396).

In terms of the neural underpinnings of these audio-visual interactions in speech perception, a number of neuroimaging studies have shown that the auditory cortex is not only activated by hearing speech sounds but also by watching lip movements and other facial articulatory gestures. In our daily lives, we tend to look at the mouth movements on the TV screen, including dramas, movies, music, and cartoons, and understand what the speaker is saying accurately. Film companies ask the sound editors to dub the voices by paying attention to the mouth movements in the original to produce voice-overs on movies. People like to watch the face of the person talking on the stage, and feel more comfortable to see than to listen to the speech on the radio without visual cues.

4.4.2. Talking faces: look and imitate

In the process of language acquisition, infants listen intently to the sound, look back and forth at a face, and try to imitate the sound. For instance, infants recognise the /a/ sounds go with mouths that are open wide, /i/ sounds with mouths that have retracted lips, and /u/ sounds with mouths whose lips are protruded and pursed. In addition, infants hearing /i/ produce sounds that are more /i/-like, while infants hearing /a/ produce sounds that are significantly /a/-like.

Speech representations, like the body transformations in facial imitation, are organised in a way that is not exclusively auditory, motor or visual, but is supramodal. This internal representation is such that an auditory signal can influence behaviour in two other modes. An auditory signal influences where infants look, causing them to look at a silent moving mouth that is phonetically equivalent to the sound they hear. The auditory signal also influences what infants say, causing them to move their mouths in a way that will result in an event that is equivalent to the one they hear (Eilan, McCarthy & Brewer, eds., 1993: 225).

Speech can be perceived by vision alone via lip

reading and visual speech perception can provide sufficient phonetic information to access the mental lexicon, so talking faces constitute a major part of an infant's perceptual experience. Through the process of watching and listening while people talk to them and point out objects of the world, infants have the opportunity to attribute semantics to the sounds they hear. The auditory and visual signals carry both complementary and redundant information on the phonetic properties of the original message.

However, the integration is something more than taking the best of both worlds, and audio-visual perception is able to perceive properties that are carried by neither modality alone. An intimate intersensory integration at the signal level comprises the dynamic aspects of both signals that are audible and visible traces of the same articulatory gestures. This intersensory integration is necessary for perception and for movement learning and control. Accurate descriptions and models of coordinate structures linking activations of the different speech segments are necessary for hearing and hearing-impaired individuals.

The latest developments in audio-visual research present computer generated facial animation, which enables speech training or computer-mediated communication to be more natural and realistic. Interaction loops between production and perception of speech and gestures are at the core of human communication, transmitting via multimodal signals parallel information about what speakers say, what they think about what they say, and how they feel when they say it. Face-to-face communication studies require the integration of embodied speech production and audio-visual speech communication and combining them with social and physical interactions between humans and between humans and their environment (Bailly, Perrier & Vatikiotis-Bateson, eds., 2012).

Optical information from facial movements of a talker contributes to speech perception not only when acoustic information is degraded or when the listener is hearing impaired, but also when the acoustic information is clearly audible. For instance, the McGurk effect occurs both when the observer is aware and when the observer is unaware of the conflicting sources of information. It unequivocally shows that visual information is used in speech perception even when auditory information is clear and undegraded (Bailly, Perrier & Vatikiotis-Bateson, eds., 2012: Chapter

4).

Recent research has shown that a foreign accent can be said to have a visual component. People are able to identify their primary language and other familiar languages from visual information. The use of visual cues to speech crucially depends on their perceived information value. The learner attends to visual information only when auditory information is degraded or absent. Integration of visual and auditory cues occurs when the observer can assume these cues contribute to a unitary perceptual event, which will depend in part on the observer's native or non-native perceptual categories.

The integration of speech information from various modalities is in part learned during the acquisition of the primary language, so that there are language-specific biases in the choice and use of visual cues to speech. The Japanese and Korean learners' identification accuracy of /f/ and /r/ increases with matched visual cues, which reveals that learners attend to visual cues to identify speech sounds. It is more efficient to incorporate into perceptual training for learners the enhancement of the information value of visual cues as a second channel of input (Leather, ed., 1999). Face-to-face communicative activities with native speakers may promote auditory and pronunciation skills.

4.4.3. Identifying location

Research revealing the inner workings of the auditory system typically uses very simple stimuli under constrained situations, often isolated pure tones heard through headphones by listeners sitting in an otherwise perfectly quiet laboratory. This is obviously not the way we experience auditory stimuli, including speech sounds in our daily lives.

Listeners use small differences in time and intensity across the two ears to learn the direction in the horizontal plane from which a sound comes, but this is not sufficient to fully indicate the location from which a sound comes, whether the sound is coming from the front or the back, or from a higher or lower elevation. The pinna, ear canal, head and torso alter the intensities of different frequencies for sounds coming from different places in space, and listeners use these changes in intensity across frequency to identify the location from which a sound comes. In everyday environments, sounds to which a person is listening often are interrupted by other sounds.

Perceptual restoration is a process by which

missing or degraded acoustic signals are perceptually replaced. Listeners make use of experience and familiarity to separate different sound sources. When we know what we are listening for, it is easier to pick out sounds from the background of other sounds.

People come to recognise a completely new sound once they have heard it a few times. Experiments have shown that although a single instance of a sound and its background was impossible to segregate, listeners could nonetheless identify the sound when it was repeated. Listeners needed only a few repetitions to perform well above chance even though they had never heard the complex sounds before (Wolfe, et al., 2012: Chapter 10).

4.4.4. Detecting and decoding emotional stimuli

Sounds from musical instruments and human vocal tracts obey the same laws of physical acoustics as all other sounds. Musical notes and spoken words are nothing more than very familiar complex sounds. In other ways, music and speech can be distinguished from other environmental sounds.

Both music and speech serve to communicate and both can convey emotion and deeper meanings. The ability to detect and accurately decode emotional stimuli arising in the environment is critical for survival. Although all sensory modalities can carry emotional information, acoustic stimuli are particularly well suited for efficiently conveying biologically relevant information. This is due to the ability of auditory stimuli to signal distant events and their rapid transmission through the nervous system.

In addition, acoustic signals are useful in communicating between members of a species. Vocalisations as well as facial expressions are relied upon extensively in intra-species communication (Rees & Palmer, eds., 2010: Chapter 19).

The final point is that visually impaired people tend to rely mainly on sounds to encode emotions, and they are revealed to be much more sensitive to sounds when it comes to mind reading. They can recognise immediately who is who by hearing his or her voice, as sighted individuals do when they see others' faces.

The following table shows the properties of sounds that evoke particular emotions (Arbib, ed., 2013: 125; Deutsch, ed., 2013: Chapter 15; Kreiman & Sidtis, 2011: Chapter 9).

Table 4-1. Acoustic cues and emotions

Emotion	Acoustic cues
Anger	• Fast speech or rate tempo • High voice intensity or sound level • Much variability in voice intensity or sound level • Much high-frequency energy • High pitch level • Much pitch variability • Rising pitch contour • Fast voice onsets or tone attacks • Microstructural irregularity
Fear	• Fast speech or rate tempo • Low voice intensity or sound level • Much variability in voice intensity or sound level • Little high-frequency energy • High pitch level • Little pitch variability • Rising pitch contour • A lot of microstructural irregularity
Happiness	• Fast speech or rate tempo • Medium high voice intensity or sound level • Medium high-frequency energy • High pitch level

	• Much pitch variability • Rising pitch contour • Fast voice onsets or tone attacks • Very little microstructural regularity
Sadness	• Slow speech or rate tempo • Low voice intensity or sound level • Little variability in voice intensity or sound level • Little high-frequency energy • Low pitch level • Little pitch variability • Falling pitch contour • Slow voice onsets or tone attacks • Microstructural irregularity
Tenderness	• Slow speech or rate tempo • Low voice intensity or sound level • Little variability in voice intensity or sound level • Little high-frequency energy • Low pitch level • Little pitch variability • Falling pitch contour • Slow voice onsets or tone attacks • Microstructural regularity

Chapter 5

Learning of Braille: reading by touch

Introduction

Reading has been called 'visible language' or 'visible speech'. To read is to understand language by means of vision. For blind people, reading by touch is the most important means of written communication. There must be 'tactile language' or 'felt speech'. Investigating how people come to understand ideas and stories from sensing Braille provides an additional source of information when sight is absent or lost later in life.

Scientific studies have shown that touch is perceptually much the same as vision as seen in Section 4.3. Reading by touch includes perceptual processes, knowledge of the language, and knowledge of the orthographic rules and conventions that govern the translation between the sounds of language and the perception of the tactual patterns that symbolise them (Millar, 1997).

In this chapter, we will have a close look at how blind people learn reading skills, the barriers they encounter, and the interrelationships among modalities.

5.1. Phonological awareness and English spelling

It has widely been considered that the ability to think about and manipulate syllables and sounds in spoken words, phonological awareness, is a necessary component of learning to read and write. Comprehending and composing written text require the integration of a wide variety of knowledge and skills, but the ability to recognise individual words in print and the ability to spell words utilising conventions that can be deciphered by the reader are central to these processes.

5.1.1. Literacy and phonological awareness

Long before children become explicitly aware of the phonological structure of words, they have developed implicit phonological knowledge that allows them to gain mastery of listening to and speaking their native language. Implicit phonological knowledge enables children to make a judgement about whether a word is part of their native language, allows for self-correction of speech errors, and enables children to discriminate between acceptable and unacceptable variations of spoken words (Gillon, 2004: Chapter 1).

Phonological awareness is a multilevel skill of breaking down words into smaller units. There are three subcategories as follows:

1. **Syllable awareness**
   Phonological awareness at syllable level requires awareness that words can be divided into syllables.
2. **Onset-rime awareness**
   Demonstrating awareness that syllables and words can be divided at the onset-rime level shows phonological awareness at the intrasyllable level. Most commonly, this level of awareness is measured through rhyming tasks.
3. **Phoneme awareness**
   A phoneme is defined as the smallest unit of sound that influences the meaning of a word, i.e. vowels and consonants. When words are spoken, the listener does not hear the separated

phonemes in words; rather, phonemes are blended into syllables within the sound stream. Individuals must learn to perceive phonemes in speech.

Phonological awareness is an individual's ability to determine the sound structure of oral language and is strongly related to literacy. In particular, phoneme awareness is a strong predictor of the level a learner has reached in reading and spelling. In order to develop phonological awareness, learners need to have reached a level of maturity in their speech perception and production skills so that when they think about their speech they are accessing consistent and reliable information about the sounds in words.

Experts in this field have widely claimed that the key foundations of literacy are phonological sensitivity and awareness (Lancaster, 2008: Chapter 4). However, some researchers propose that phonological awareness skills develop only after one experiences a written form of language and develops the ability to recognise written letters.

Beginning readers of Braille are expected to develop phonological awareness skills in the same manner as readers of print. Most literacy activities have a very strong listening aspect, but particularly important during the elementary/introductory level is the ability to hear and distinguish sounds as they are paired with Braille symbols. Memory plays an important role in this process.

Millar (1997: Chapter 4) suggests that phonological recoding is more prevalent in Braille than in visual reading, especially for beginners. Short-term memory is involved in learning and reading Braille, but recall spans are much longer for phonologically recoded than for tactually coded patterns. Memory for sounds is more important in the initial stages of learning to read Braille than print, because Braille patterns are associated from the onset with heard sounds rather than mediated via pictures of objects. Attention to speech sounds is necessarily more important for blind people than for the sighted.

Listening skills related to literacy include the following (Barclay, 2012: Chapter 4):

1. Discriminate and identify verbal and nonverbal sounds.
2. Demonstrate understanding of spoken words, syllables and sounds.
3. Know and apply grade-level phonics and word

analysis skills in decoding words.
4. Ask and answer questions about key details in a text read aloud or information presented orally or through other media.
5. Select the main idea, summarise, relate one idea to another, and make inferences.
6. Recount or describe key ideas or details from a text read aloud or information presented orally or through other media.
7. Connect literary texts to personal experiences and previously encountered texts to enhance understanding and appreciation.

5.1.2. Complexity of spelling rules

At this point, let us look briefly at English spelling. No one who reads any passage of English can fail to notice the frequent mismatch between the sounds of English and the letters used to record them. English has frequently been criticised for the complexity of its spelling rules and for the lack of a system and consistency in the relationship between the sounds of the spoken language and the symbols of the written language. Given that in many languages, including Japanese hiragana and katakana, there is a clear and predictable relationship between speech sounds and the written characters that represent them, learners might well ask why this is not the case with English. According to Upward & Davidson (2011), the answer lies in the history of the English language, and they trace that history in so far as it pertains to the development of modern English spelling and its relationship to modern English pronunciation.

However, there are philologists and lexicographers who express their doubts about the commonly assumed self-evident axiom that a phonetic spelling must necessarily be the most suitable for any language without regard to its character or history. It may be advantageous for orthography to deviate from a phonetically faithful representation of speech and that various non-phonological factors need to be taken account of in spelling (Upward & Davidson, 2011: 310).

One of the non-phonological factors that needs to be considered is what is called communicative clarity. Written language is generally employed in situations where the communicator and the person being communicated with are not present at the same place and time, and it is necessary that there be as little scope for confusion and misunderstanding as possible. Homophones, words that are the same in sound (for example, rite/right, male/mail, sine/sign, etc.), present less possibility for confusion than do homographs, words that are the same in their written forms, and for this reason a spelling system that allows homographs is arguably to be preferred to one which does not. This is true to the kanji system in Japanese as well.

Secondly, English is spoken in a large number of different accents with very different sound patterns. A spelling system that is designed to represent accurately the pronunciation of one accent will almost certainly fail to represent accurately pronunciation in at least some of the other accents. A narrowly sound-based spelling system could accommodate the difference.

Thirdly, a rigidly phonetic spelling system would lose many of the visual connections between related words, such as photograph and photographer, injury and injurious, nature and natural, etc. There is arguably something to be said in favour of a spelling system that makes words that are related in meaning graphically alike. Similarly, in a spelling system with complete consistency in sound-symbol correspondences, valuable features of symbol-meaning correspondence might be lost. For instance, the visual relationship between -s and plurality will be lost.

The major factor affecting English spelling today, which may have implications for the future of the spelling system, is the influence of electronic modes of communication. The electronic medium is a much more immediate means of communication and messages are written quickly without careful attention to details of grammar, spelling and punctuation. Electronic communication draws upon shortened forms of common words and an established set of abbreviations (Horobin, 2013: Chapter 8).

5.2. Processing of Braille

Braille is a well-known tactile substitution for visual letter forms for the blind, which consists of a series of raised dots that can be read with the fingers. Braille symbols are formed within units of space known as Braille cells. A full Braille cell consists of six raised dots arranged in two parallel columns, each having three dots. Sixty-three combinations are possible using one or more of these six dots. A single cell can be used to represent a letter of the alphabet, a number, a mathematical sign, a punctuation mark, music, or even a whole word. Braille is a code by which languages, such as English and Japanese, can be written and read.

Braille has become a worldwide standard as an effective means of communication as well as a proven avenue for achieving and enhancing literacy for the blind (Sadato, 2005).

Blind learners use touch independently to gain information. This is called 'active touch', which includes haptic exploration/perception and tactile reading. Exploration of raised symbols through touch and vision is schematised as follows (McLinden & McCall, 2002: Chapter 3):

| Vision | → | Spatial examination of visual form | → | Information processing |

| Touch | → | Serial/linear examination of tactile structure | → | Information processing |

Braille is the most successful system for the transmission of written information to the blind. In this method, visual perception of printed characters is replaced by tactile interpretation of raised dots. Braille requires a complex mental process involving finger movement control, dot perception, pattern recognition, and lexical and syntactic processing.

5.2.1. Guiding principles

Guidelines on which to base phonological awareness training can be derived from research findings (Gillon, 2004: Chapter 7). Note that these statements are meaningful in the first language environment, where learners have already acquired sound systems of their first language. In a foreign language learning environment, it is necessary for them to learn their target language through sounds first in order to develop phonological awareness of the foreign language.

1. Phonological awareness training should be integrated with letter-sound knowledge training and should make explicit the links between speech and Braille.
2. Phonological awareness training should focus on the development of skills at the phoneme level for learners.
3. An individual or small group model of service delivery may be necessary for learners with severe deficits.
4. Flexibility in programme implementation is required, and phonological awareness training is most effective after a period of general language learning.

5. Suggested Braille learning proceeds as follows:

5.2.2. Contractions

Contractions constitute the most notable orthographic difference between English Braille and print.

Uncontracted Braille, called Grade 1, is an easy and straightforward way to code printed words into a tactile format. Each letter converted into uncontracted Braille takes up around the same space as a letter in 24 point Arial font. As a result, uncontracted Braille requires extra time for the reader to process it.

On the other hand, contracted Braille, Grade 2, is a compact form of Braille designed to save reading time and space, making reading Braille more efficient and convenient. Some contractions represent phonetic combinations such as 'ch', 'sh', 'th', or 'wh', while others represent letter clusters like 'ed', 'in', 'ing', 'con', 'dis' or 'tion'. The word 'and' would be spelled with only one Braille character, while 'band' would have two characters, one for 'b' and one for 'and'. It can be partially contracted, in which some letters or symbols can represent a word or a preposition.

In addition, it can be fully contracted: a

combination of letters representing words, as well as one symbol, can stand for two letters, for example, 'st' or 'er'. Words can be shortened by contracting some syllables; for example, the word 'comfortable' is comprised of three contracted symbols for 'com', 'for' and 'ble' but individual letters for 'ta'. The contraction 'in' is found in the word 'inn' spelled 'in' + 'n', and in the word 'dined' spelled 'd' + 'in' + 'ed'. The contraction for 'the' is used for the words THEir, THEm, furTHEr, and caTHEdral. More concrete examples can be found in Figure 5-2.

Contractions often bear no resemblance to the letters for which they stand, referring to orthographic units and not sound units. Contractions often cut across phonological boundaries such as syllables as well. Visually impaired children find it harder to analyse contracted Braille, and need additional time to work out contractions. This is because many of the contractions cannot be identified using phonetic and phonological knowledge. Some researchers and teachers have argued that it takes longer to read contracted Braille. Dodd & Conn (2000) claim that contractions may interfere with blind children's ability to detect phonemes in words, and consequently their reading and spelling ability.

The question whether contractions save time as well as space does not have a simple answer. Contractions that represent whole words when standing alone do save processing time. Familiar words or frequent words that contain contractions are processed faster in terms of time per character than the same words spelt out in full. The advantage depends on lexical knowledge and frequent activation (Millar, 1997: Chapter 6).

Table 5-1. Learning to read written forms

Normal-sighted children:
Acquisition of sound patterns → Alphabetic writing system → Linking sound and letter rules

Blind children:
Acquisition of sound patterns → Braille and alphabetic writing systems → Linking sound and Braille rules including contractions together with fully spelt-out equivalent

5.2.3. Transfer

It has been claimed that, in striking contrast to its simple sound system, the Japanese language employs what is arguably the most convoluted writing system ever devised in human history. This notoriety is ultimately due to the fact that Japanese writing evolved from that of Chinese, a language with substantially different sound and word formation systems. In the late fourth and fifth centuries, Chinese script was introduced to Japan. In Chinese, each meaning unit consisted of one syllable and was represented by a single character called a kanji.

Recording a language with kanji is fundamentally different from doing it with the Roman alphabet, which is designed to represent speech sounds. In kanji writing, ideas rather than sounds are represented, associated with one or more strings of sounds and the letter-sound association is secondary to the representation of ideas. Hiragana and katakana represent the Japanese sound system, but kanji is frequently used in Japanese texts nowadays. In addition, the Hepburn System, based on English writing conventions, is used widely (Hasegawa, 2015: Chapter 4).

Blind students need to learn letter-sound association of Japanese by means of Braille based on hiragana, and then the Hepburn System with the English Braille system.

Interferences of Braille systems have not been discussed widely in the literature. These phenomena are very common among beginners and some intermediate blind students who are learning English. Many blind pupils learn Japanese Braille at primary school, and then they start learning the English Braille system at secondary school, because English language learning is compulsory in Japan.

As the figures show, Japanese and English Braille codes use the same dot arrangements, but they represent completely different letters and sounds, which causes serious learning problems. For instance, English Braille for 'apple' is read as /a-ne-ne-ni-go/ in Japanese Braille. Some students remember English spelling as a learning strategy by referring to Japanese sounds that are completely different. This phenomenon seems to be peculiar to Braille readers who use a non-alphabetic writing system like Japanese.

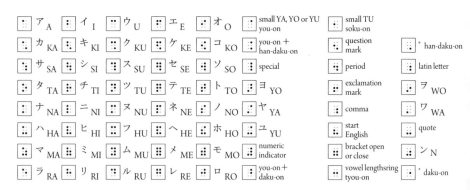

Figure 5-1. Japanese Braille code (Reprinted by permission from RNIB)

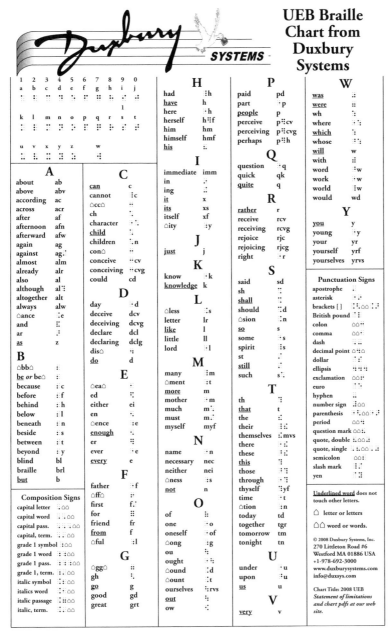

Figure 5-2. English Braille (Reprinted by permission from Duxbury Systems, Inc.)

English teachers and learners have been struggling with mastering English Braille systems, including the Grade 2 Braille system. They spend many years to learn them, but ironically, they do not have time to learn listening and speaking skills for communication. Students find English learning extremely stressful and tough, because some students are forced to just practise the complicated Braille systems all the time. To make matters worse, as English is not spoken in Japan, students seldom hear English sounds, while native speakers of English acquire sounds first and then learn Braille. We will discuss this problem further in Chapter 8.

In the field of literacy, it is widely known that listening does not take the place of reading, but rather, effective listening skills support the development of literacy. Kuhn & Levy (2015) clearly state that fluent reading consists of automaticity (instantaneous recognition of words in text without conscious effort or attention) and prosody (the stress, emphasis and phrasing that create an expressive rendering of a text). In fact, the development of listening skills is essential to the development of literacy skills. Most researchers and authorities agree that learners with well-developed listening and speaking language skills find it easier to read and write in the first and second languages (Barclay, 2012: Chapter 1). This basic requirement is not fulfilled in English language teaching in Japan.

Table 5-2. Braille for foreign languages

Traditional approach
Learning the English Braille system by learning pronunciation altogether → Memorise spellings → Practice reading
Suggested approach
Getting used to English sound system first → Connecting English sounds with Braille → Practice reading

5.3. Writing/producing Braille

Writing is a tool that people have developed to help circumvent a limitation of spoken language. Using writing, people can convey information to others who are remote in time and space. Learning to write is a prerequisite for being a full member of a literate society. Writing the individual words correctly and following other orthographic conventions, such as the use of proper punctuation, are an important part of the writing process. Learning about a writing system allows one to use that writing system. Mentally spelling a new word helps someone remember it or writing down an address allows one to avoid the trouble of memorising it (Treiman & Kessler, 2014: Chapter 13).

The use of most technological aids requires learners to acquire keyboard skills and touch typing. Webster & Roe (1998: Chapter 5) suggest that children of pre-school age can be given a pre-Braille programme to develop the finger strength and coordination necessary to operate a Perkins Braille Writer. They can enjoy making dot patterns and writing pretend messages whilst also developing finger strength and familiarising themselves with the Braille keys.

About 25% of braillists still make use of the stylus and hand frame for taking notes, but mechanical Braille writing devices are available nowadays. The Perkins Braille Writer is still probably the most commonly used device for writing at school. The Perkins is a mechanical writer that has six keys, each key corresponding to a dot in the Braille cell. When the keys are pressed down in the appropriate combination, raised letters and signs are embossed onto on a sheet of manila Braille paper that is fed manually into the machine.

In recent years, a variety of electronic Braille writing devices have been developed, which also make use of the six-key format for input. Output may take the form of synthetic speech or a constantly renewable/refreshable tactile display on the machine itself (Mason & McCall, eds., 1997: Chapter 16).

For many blind learners, reading Braille can be a slow process, since the tactile reader can only read one Braille cell at a time, and is unable to scan a line of print. Blind people learning to read and write using Braille must rely on tactual spatial abilities and auditory skills. Spelling is a difficult task for blind learners, who must master words using word signs, contractions and abbreviations and yet must also learn the full spelling of a word for typing to produce a print copy (Mason & McCall, eds., 1997: Chapter 10).

At an early stage of learning spelling and writing, sighted and blind learners need activities that promote what they are able to do with explicit spelling system knowledge (Hayes & Flanigan, 2014: 121).

Table 5-3. From reading to spelling

Phonological awareness	• Isolate and produce the initial, medial vowel, and final sounds (phonemes) in three phoneme (consonant vowel consonant) words. • Distinguish long from short vowel sounds in spoken single-syllable words. • Orally produce single-syllable words by blending sounds (phonemes), including consonant blends. • Add or substitute individual sounds (phonemes) in simple, one-syllable words to make new words. • Segment spoken single-syllable words into their complete sequence of individual sounds (phonemes).
Phonics and word recognition	• Read common high-frequency words. Know the spelling-sound correspondences for common consonant digraphs. • Decode regularly spelled one-syllable words. • Read words with inflectional endings. • Recognise and read irregularly spelled words.

Spelling	• Spell simple words phonetically, drawing on knowledge of sound-letter relationships.
	• Conventional spelling for words with common spelling patterns.

It is much harder for blind students to learn writing skills than normally sighted students, because Braille writer instruction is required. Ease and fluency in correct fingering are prerequisites to the development of speed and accuracy in writing Braille. If each key on the Braille writer is identified by a number according to the dot which it forms and each finger is identified by a number according to the key it should press, the beginning writer is encouraged to maintain accurate finger position on the keys. The dot numbers provide the best description of any configuration. This description is applicable when referring to the embossed character, to the position of fingers upon the writer keys, or to the formation of symbols with the slate and stylus (Harley, et al., 1997: Chapter 8).

Although Braille provides blind students with a method for writing, Braille writing is slow, and it is very difficult to correct errors and communicate the errors to the students. Some researchers propose that word processing offers an invaluable tool for improving their writing skills and communicating their ideas. Word processing makes writing easier for students by providing them with the ability to do what sighted students usually do. This idea presupposes that blind students should read Braille but write full spellings without contractions, i.e. print literacy. Nowadays, a variety of technology is available which can make computers accessible to blind people. This accessible technology, including Braille displays, Braille embossers, speech synthesisers, and screen readers, enables them to use word processing as a method of writing.

Reading and writing tasks require skill in every aspect of perception. Learners who are blind or visually impaired may be having academic difficulties related to perception. An essential component of storing and retrieving information in memory is that the information must be perceived and recalled in the same sequential pattern.

According to Harley (1997: Chapter 6), perceptual errors commonly made by students with visual impairments have been grouped into seven types listed below. These errors are widespread among foreign language learners as well as native speakers of

English. The perceptual errors in reading and writing are rarely random errors. Usually there is a pattern of errors in perception that prompts the learner to choose a particular response.

1. **Reversals (mirrored writing; retrography)**

    Some students with visual limitations write letters with a reverse horizontal orientation. Common left-right reversals in print are 'b' for 'd' and 'p' for 'q'. For the Braille student, common reversals are 'e' for 'i', 'f' for 'd', and 'ing' for 'u'. A reader with a visual impairment may reverse the shapes of letters and the order of the letters within the word. For instance, a Braille student may read the word 'friend', which is represented in Braille by the letters 'fr', as the word 'would', which is written in Braille by the letters 'wd'. In this case, each letter is reversed as well as the sequence of letters. A significant reversal problem may cause exchange of the sequence of words and concepts as well as letter shapes and order. A student may read and/or write 'dig' for 'big', 'dug' for 'bug', 'no' for 'on', or 'Tim' for 'Jim'.

2. **Inversions**

    Letters may be written or read in a reverse vertical

orientation. A few of these rotations in print are 'u' for 'n' and 'w' for 'm'. In Braille, a typical inversion is 'u' for 'm' or 'f' for 'h'. Both reversals and inversions are more common in Braille than in print because of the numerous meaningful reversals and inversions possible in Braille.

3. **Transpositions**

    The reordering of items within a sequence is a transposition. Common errors are 'who' for 'how', or 'stop' for 'spot'. A common error made by Braille readers in which letters are reordered is reading 'on' for 'now'. Such misperceptions involve the reordering of letters either at the receptive level of memory or in the storage and retrieval of information. The student may be transposing the beginning and end of a word when reading 'play' for 'help', or 'said' for 'and'.

4. **Omissions**

    Students may omit letters in words or omit whole words in sentences as they read or write. The writing errors may contain omitted letters and syllables similar to their omissions in reading. The most frequently omitted letters are the vowels. Entire syllables may be omitted. The way these students misspell words will closely approximate the way they pronounce them. For example, a student may say and spell 'enfirment' for 'environment'. Students may omit endings when writing words and omit words and punctuation when writing sentences. Students with visual impairment attempt to identify a word by focusing only on the middle or end of the word rather than the beginning. This type of mistake is a perceptual error involving omitted letters. Such errors include 'way' for 'away', or 'cake' for 'make'.

5. **Substitutions**

    Students may commonly substitute one word for another as they read and write. Substitution errors predominate over other errors. For example, a student frequently substitutes 'the' and 'they' in writing, because the words 'they' and 'the' are both formed in Braille or print by similar symbols. Other cases are substitution of 'list' for 'lost', 'mess' for 'miss', 'slaps' for 'sleeps', or 'cape' for 'cake'. Students tend not to recognise their own errors. It is important to determine whether they are visual/tactile or auditory substitutions.

6. **Insertions**

    Perceptual learning difficulties may cause students to insert additional letters of words as they read or write. Repetitions are also insertions of a type, in that the repeated word is inserted into the flow of words and disrupts the context of reading or writing. Frequently, the inserted letter forms an initial or final blend in the error word. The most commonly inserted letters are 'l' and 'r'. These inserted letters are common to Braille readers. Insertion of 'l' or 'r' produces errors such as 'black' for 'back', 'frog' for 'fog', or 'grown' for 'gown'. Frequently, the error word is more familiar to the student than the actual word.

7. **Sequencing**
Moving back and forth within a sequence is another aspect of sequential perception and memory. Students are confused by time requirements, and may not be able to sequence events in order.

5.4. Cross-modal plasticity

The human sensory system allows individuals to perceive the natural environment and maintain situation awareness during complex, dynamic tasks. The human brain can use multiple sensory channels to perceive the contextual data needed to disambiguate incomplete or illusory data provided by any single sense (Hoffman, et al., eds., 2015: Chapters 15 & 17).

Visual and tactile information is relayed from the eyes or the skin to the brain along physically separate pathways. At the level of the cerebral cortex, there are separate primary areas that process information independently for vision and touch, known as the primary visual cortex and the primary somatosensory cortex, respectively. Although the merging of visual and somatosensory information takes place in higher-order cortical areas, such processing is dependent on the primary cortical areas (Sadato, 2005).

A number of characteristics of objects have been the focus of perception research. The sense of touch is of major importance for the perception of three-dimensional objects. A prominent property of many objects is curvature, and volume is a measure of the size of objects. The haptic perception of weight is subject to illusions: a smaller object with the same weight as a larger object will be perceived as heavier. The haptic perception of texture is induced by the surface properties of objects, which can be thought of as consisting of roughness and friction. Several aspects of the material of which an object is made can be perceived haptically. The surface properties of the material determine the object's texture, including compliance, the ease with which the object can be deformed under pressure, and thermal properties, the rate at which heat is extracted from the hand when the object is touched.

Braille reading requires the conversion of simple tactile information into meaningful patterns that have lexical and semantic properties. While the perceptual processing of Braille may be mediated by the somatosensory system, visual letter identity is routinely accomplished within the visual system. The spatial information originally conveyed by the tactile pathway in sighted people from the primary to the secondary somatosensory area might be processed by the neuronal networks usually reserved for the visual shape discrimination process in the blind (Sadato, et al., 1998). There is psychological evidence that spatial coding depends on the integration and organisation of multimodal inputs. Both touch and visual systems code for shape. Absence of vision biases inputs for shape information toward touch, and the visual cortex is freed for processing tactile information in the blind.

More precisely, Sadato et al. (2002) propose that in blind people, whose bottom-up visual processing is interrupted, tactile shape discrimination processing expands into the visual association cortex. In early onset, but not late onset, blind people, the primary visual cortex is recruited in a functionally relevant way, as in top-down processing during visual imagery, which results in better performance on shape discrimination in early onset blind people. Visual and tactile processing is competitively balanced in the occipital cortex. During the execution of tasks with a significant tactile element, deafferented areas of the visual cortex are recruited in the blind, but not in the sighted. Sadato et al. (2004) suggest that this recruitment is not a learning-related phenomenon but rather due to sensory influences. Long-term visual deafferentation can improve tactile acuity independent of prior Braille learning, possibly due to plasticity in the occipital cortex.

More recently, Landau ed. (2013: Chapter 4) has presented compelling studies of cognition in the congenitally blind, using data from behavioural and brain imaging studies to explore how lifelong absence of visual experience affects cognitive structure and function. Extensive evidence now shows that the primary visual cortex in congenitally blind people can take on other sensory/perceptual functions, e.g. special functions underlying the perception of Braille, as well as high-level functions involved in language.

Given this significant evidence supporting plasticity of the human brain in its basic organisation, and its dependence on particular types of sensory experience, the author asks whether the same plasticity effects extend to higher-level functions such as concepts. Blind and sighted individuals possess much the same conceptual structures for lexical concepts; moreover, these structures are housed in virtually identical areas of the brain for the blind and sighted.

Brain regions with strong innate biases have a dramatic capacity for change. In children who grow up without sight, visual circuits develop drastically different cognitive functions. The same brain regions that support visuo-spatial discrimination in sighted people participate in abstract cognitive functions such as language in blind individuals. Visual cortex plasticity demonstrates the pluripotency of human neural circuits during development. While developmental blindness profoundly reorganises brain regions that encode the surface structure of the visual world, it leaves the neurobiology of concepts largely unchanged. Even in the case of concrete categories of objects and actions, blind people know similar information and this information is implemented in similar neural systems.

To summarise, the role of the primary visual cortex for Braille readers is to support Braille reading activities. The visual cortex is activated to process tactile information and the somatosensory area of the brain has less activation during Braille reading among blind people.

5.5. Perceptual limitations and aging

In this section, we discuss age-related changes in perception. We should note that haptics, audition, and vision changes often co-occur (Hoffman, et al., 2015: Chapter 51).

The sense of touch is referred to as haptic or tactile ability. Older adults can experience declines in haptic acuity, distance discrimination, and temporal processing. Age-related declines in haptic processing may result in challenges in dealing with technology. Such declines may make it more difficult for older adults to manipulate buttons, keyboards, and touch screens as well as limit their ability to perceive haptic feedback and output from devices.

Haptic or tactile acuity has been shown to decrease with age. It is estimated that the tactile acuity of adults diminishes by one percent each year after the age of twenty. There are differential losses in sensitivity with age, with more loss occurring in general in the lower limbs than the upper limbs.

Hearing is often required to interact fully with people and devices. Older people commonly experience auditory declines, including losses in acuity, frequency discrimination, and temporal processing. Presbycusis is the loss of hearing attributed to age-related changes. Nearly 46 percent of adults aged over 45 years experience hearing loss, and this increases to about 90 percent of adults over the age of eighty. Men are more susceptible to hearing loss than women because of more exposure to occupational noise.

Age-related changes can result in adults' decreased abilities to discriminate sound frequencies. These deficits affect comprehension of speech as well as discrimination of sounds. Presbycusis impacts higher frequencies earlier in life and to a greater extent than lower frequencies. Above the age of thirty, men experience hearing loss twice as much as women at most ages and frequencies. The higher frequencies of human speech (about 4000 Hz) as well as high-frequency non-speech sounds may be inaudible to older adults. For instance, higher-frequency voices of women and children and high-frequency beeps, pings, and alerts can be more difficult or impossible for older adults to hear.

Adults experience decreased abilities in temporal processing, including the ability to discriminate durations of sounds and temporal gaps between sounds. Age-related declines in temporal processing can be particularly problematic for comprehending faster rates of speech. In addition, background noise and reverberation limit adults' comprehension of auditory information. Age-related deficits for speech recognition and comprehension in noise depend on many factors, such as the capacities of the listener, audibility of speech, type of speech, signal-to-noise ratio, and type of noise.

As most sighted people know, adults experience limitations in visual acuity, contrast sensitivity, and colour discrimination as well as difficulties with glare and identifying items in complex or changing scenes. These age-related declines affect the ability to process visual information.

Approximately 70 percent of severely vision-impaired adults above the age of sixty-five also demonstrate significant hearing loss. Given the prevalence of dual sensory impairment, multimodal input/output and feedback options may be particularly important for making technologies accessible for users. Haptic and auditory feedback can be used to support visual perception.

Millar (1997) clearly states that the assumption that there is a 'sensitive period' for learning Braille is too simplistic. As we saw, tactile sensitivity, like all the senses, including vision and hearing, deteriorates with age, meaning that one's senses of hearing, sight and touch are less acute in old age. But there is evidence that Braille readers who have learned Braille from the start and have used it constantly remain good Braille readers even in old age. The question is more about what is learned first and what has received most practice. People who go blind later, i.e. after having learned print (or Japanese characters) first, have to change from Japanese characters to Braille, and are likely to have learned the new subjects for less time, and often with less teaching help and repetition than children who have learned the system at school and used it continuously for all subjects.

However, if they are sufficiently motivated to and want to master Braille, they can learn to read even difficult literature, and remain literate even if they may not be as fast. Some of the evidence is given by Millar (1997). Overall, tactile 'sensitivity' is less important than good strategies in lateral scanning across Braille characters. This is true for listening and speaking skills as well. We will discuss the significance of exposure to language and frequency of use as crucial factors in Chapters 7 and 8.

Chapter 6

Cognitive and linguistic characteristics

Introduction

Many people think of blindness as the total absence of visual sensation, and they imagine that a blind person is someone who experiences the world through a kind of black void. In fact, blindness cannot be viewed in terms of an absolute dichotomy between the presence and absence of visual information. The popular conception of the blind person characterises only a very small proportion of the blind population, since the vast majority of blind individuals experience and utilise some visual information (Dunlea, 1989: 7).

Because of its importance to us, we surmise that the absence of vision must have devastating consequences and that congenital blindness must inevitably lead to the construction of a rather different perspective of the world. Vision enables us to establish and maintain a coherent concept of the environment and our existence in it without struggling with memory and information retrieval.

The blind must remember what the sighted can effortlessly reconstruct with a single look. The blind build up concepts of the world based on auditory, tactual and kinaesthetic experiences. Hearing is primarily useful as a means of verbal communication and in locomotion, but perception of spatial qualities of objects can only be achieved by touch in which kinaesthetic sensations participate (Dunlea, 1989: 10).

The main focus of this chapter is on the cognitive and linguistic development of the blind. We will define the notion of concepts first and review what has been proposed about the acquisition of concepts. Blind people acquire concepts and language by means of the senses of hearing and touch, and linguistic definitions/usage.

6.1. Concepts and mental representations

Concepts are one of the most fundamental constructs in theories of the mind. Given their importance to all aspects of cognition, concepts raise so many controversies in philosophy and cognitive science. Human beings come to possess a rich conceptual understanding of the world: understanding formulated in terms of such concepts as sanctity, electron, infinity or galaxy. Different types of processes underlie the formation of our conceptual repertoire. They are operating over individual learning, historical or cultural construction, and evolution. Some concepts arise in some form over evolutionary time, and other concepts spring from human cultures; the construction process must be understood in terms of both the learning mechanism and sociocultural processes of human individuals (Carey, 2009: 3).

Our perception of reality is shaped by the activity patterns of neuronal groups within the brain that help form a state of mind. These groups are clustered into functional units capable of representing experiences in different modalities, such as sight or taste, words or sensations, abstract ideas or perceptual images. The ways individuals assemble particular neuronal activities within themselves or in interaction with other people determine the nature of their subjective experiences of reality. Under this line of thinking, communication can be viewed within human relationships in part as the ways in which these mental representations are shared (Siegel, 2012: Chapter 6).

6.1.1. What are concepts?

Concepts are units of thought, the constituents of beliefs and theories, and the concepts of interest are roughly the grain of single lexical items. The representations of word meanings are paradigm examples of concepts. Representations are states of the nervous system that have content, that refer to concrete or abstract entities, properties, and events. The mental representation that encapsulates the commonalities and structure that exist among items within categories is generally referred to as a concept. In cognitive science, a concept refers to a mentally possessed idea or notion, whereas a category refers to set of entities that are grouped together. For instance, the concept 'DOG' is whatever psychological state signifies thoughts of dogs, and the category 'dog' consists of all the entities in the external world that are appropriately categorised as dogs. In short, concepts are in minds while categories are sets in the external world (Rakison & Oakes, eds., 2003: Chapter 16).

Categorisation is only possible if the respective categories are in some way available in the cognitive system. In the terminology of cognitive science, categorisation requires mental representation of the categories. Categories are represented by concepts for their exemplars. The category 'dog' is represented in the mind by the concept 'DOG'. When we encounter an object, our cognitive apparatus will produce a preliminary description of it, which consists of what we perceive of the object, such things as size, shape, colour, and smell. The description will be compared with the concepts we have in our mind, and if the description happens to match with the concept 'DOG', the object will be categorised as a 'dog'.

Table 6-1. Forms of representations

Sensory representations	Sensation and perception: sight, hearing, olfaction, taste and touch
Conceptual/categorical representations	Mind's creation of ideas and notions of the mind itself
Linguistic representations	Socially shared packets called words

As Jackendoff (2012: Chapter 10) clearly states, the possibility that meanings of words and sentences might be visual images rather than definitions in terms of words will not work. A single image of an object, such as a dog, whether we imagine it or draw it, is too particular to stand for all the different ways the object can look, and the visual image cannot tell us what is important to pay attention to, what meaning is supposed to be conveyed.

When we recognise something in the visual environment as an instance of a particular type we know, the following processing happens (Jackendoff, 2012: Chapter 23):

1. In the act of perceiving the object, our mind generates a visual surface and a spatial structure in response to the environment.
2. The spatial structure in turn is linked to a conceptual structure that says this is a particular object (token).
3. The combination of a spatial structure and conceptual structure is matched up with the concept of the object in general, stored in our long-term memory. This concept consists of a spatial structure, which encodes what it looks like, linked to a conceptual structure that says this is a type of object with some properties.
4. The conceptual structure in turn is linked to the phonological word in long-term memory.

The only parts of this process that reach consciousness are visual surface and the phonological word (pronunciation); thus, as far as we are aware, seeing something is much simpler. Token concepts can come about because of what we perceive. We learn various things go together in a category of objects, such as dogs. Learning a category amounts to our mind constructing a type of concept in response to sample tokens.

We can understand things in the world as belonging to categories only because our minds construct the categories. What our mind constructs mostly consists of spatial and conceptual structures that are not cognitive correlates of consciousness. We can tell whether things belong to the category or not without knowing exactly how we do it, because the concept we have constructed is unconscious, and only its effects in judging tokens are conscious.

Word meanings do not coincide with our concepts for actual categories. For example, the word car is a relatively abstract concept that is just rich enough for defining the category of cars, but one will have a richer concept depending on his/her individual knowledge of cars and his/her personal experiences. The concept that constitutes the meaning of the word is only part of the concept in one's mind that defines his/her personal category of cars. The meaning of the word must be a much leaner concept that is shared by all speakers who know the word and its meaning.

In addition, we do not have a word for every category we have a concept for. There are infinitely many concepts that can be expressed only by complex expressions. There are categories and concepts that cannot be verbalised at all or only insufficiently. Many concepts for bodily sensations, feelings, emotions, facial expressions and physiognomies, flavours and odours, and harmonies can hardly be put into words. The system of lexical meanings is only part of the overall system of concepts, and a lexicalised concept is only part of the richer concept that defines the category we actually connect to the word (Lobner, 2013: Chapter 11).

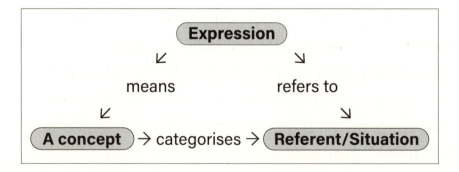

Concepts can be seen as a way of talking about the basic constituents of thought. Without concepts, there would be no thoughts. Concepts are basic timber of our mental lives. Riemer (2010: Chapter 1) states that the hypothesis that meanings are concepts has considerable attraction. It answers to the intuition that language is intimately connected with the rest of our mental lives. It does seem precisely to be because of the thoughts and concepts we have that we use the words we use. Language and thought are very hard to tease apart. Whether or not we always think in language, we often need to use language to externalise the results of our thought.

Concepts have the form of symbolic mental representations. Mental representations are the fixed mental symbols that are instantiated in our minds in some stable finite medium, and that our thought consists in. Thinking and expressing meaning are both to be understood as the manipulation of mental symbols.

Linguistically, the meanings of words and sentences can be summed up as follows: the meaning of a content word is a concept that provides a mental description of a certain kind of entity, and the meaning of a sentence is a concept that provides a mental description of a certain kind of situation. The processes that determine conceptual content fall into two broad classes: causal mechanisms that connect a mental representation to the entities in the world in its extension, and computational processes internal to the mind that determine how the representation functions in thought (Carey, 2009: 5).

Concepts are situated at the very centre of cognitive science and are hotly debated by linguists, philosophers, psychologists and others. Margolis & Laurence (1999: Chapter 1) summarise the major theories of concepts as follows:

Table 6-2. Theories of concepts

The Classical Theory

Most concepts are structured mental representations that encode a set of necessary and sufficient conditions for their application, if possible, in sensory or perceptual terms.

Criticisms:

There are few examples of defined concepts. In particular, lexical concepts show no effects of definitional structure in psychological experiments. Furthermore, it is possible to have a concept in spite of massive ignorance or error, so concept possession cannot be a matter of knowing a definition.

The Prototype Theory

Most concepts are structured mental representations that encode the properties that objects in their extension tend to possess.

Criticisms:

Typicality effects do not argue for prototype structure, since even well-defined concepts exhibit typicality effects. Many concepts lack prototypes or exemplars. In addition, concepts with prototype structure fail to cover highly atypical instances and incorrectly include non-instances. The prototypes of complex concepts are not generally a function of the prototype of their constituent concepts.

The Theory Theory

Concepts are representations whose structure consists in their relations to other concepts as specified by a mental theory.

Criticisms:

It is possible to have a concept in spite of its being tied up with a deficient or erroneous mental theory. The content of a concept cannot remain invariant across changes in its mental theory. The mechanisms that are responsible for the emergence of new scientific theories and for the shift from one theory to another are poorly understood.

The Neoclassical Theory

Most concepts are structured mental representations that encode partial definitions, i.e. necessary conditions for their application.

Criticisms:

If partial definitions are turned into full definitions, then the Neoclassical Theory has all the problems that are associated with the Classical Theory. If they are left incomplete, the Neoclassical Theory has no account of reference determination. Furthermore, Neoclassical structure cannot explain how a word retains aspects of its meaning across different semantic fields. Either its conceptual constituents must themselves have Neoclassical structure or no structure is needed at all.

Conceptual Atomism

Lexical concepts are primitive, and they have no structure.

Criticisms:

Under Conceptual Atomism, most lexical concepts turn out to be innate. If lexical concepts are primitive, they cannot explain psychological phenomena such as categorisation, so they lack an adequate explanation of why people have intuitions of analyticity.

6.1.2. Core cognition and representations

Recent cognitive approaches to cognition hypothesise

that there are two types of conceptual representations: those embedded in systems of core cognition and those embedded in an explicit knowledge system. Learning processes are characterised as those that build representations of the world on the basis of computations on input that is itself representational, including operant conditioning, connectionist supervised and unsupervised learning algorithms, and habituation.

Regarding the genetically determined aspects of concepts, claiming that representations of red or round are innate does not require that the child have some mental representation of red or round in the absence of experience with red or round things. The capacity for forming colour or shape representations could be innate even though no representations of colours or shapes are ever activated until entities are processed by sensory mechanisms. In addition, human beings have the capacity to create representational systems that transcend sensory representations and core cognition. Human beings create new representational sources that are qualitatively different from the representations they are built from.

According to Carey (2009: Chapter 3), core cognition has several properties. First, core cognition has rich integrated conceptual content. The representations in core cognition cannot be reduced to perceptual or sensori-motor primitives, the representations are accessible and drive voluntary action, and representations from distinct core cognition systems interact in central inferential processes. Second, core cognition is articulated in terms of representations that are created by innate perceptual input analysers. Natural selection has constructed these analysers specifically for the purpose of representing certain classes of entities in the world, and these analysis devices that identify the entities that fall under core domains continue to operate throughout life.

Core cognition is elaborated during development because core cognition systems are learning devices. They are not overturned or lost, in contrast to later developing explicit knowledge, which are sometimes replaced by subsequent incommensurable ones. The innate input analysers create representations of numbers and agencies of core cognition.

6.1.3. Explicit knowledge and representations

People pick up many patterns in the world through statistical learning. Much of this knowledge is implicit, in the sense that it is tacit and hard to verbalise. Children who have learned about the statistics of their environment may respond more quickly or more accurately to a common event than an uncommon one, and they may be able to predict the next event in a sequence. However, people may be unable to report on the structure that drives their behaviour, sometimes even denying that a pattern exists. When people provide verbal reports about what they know implicitly, those reports may be incomplete and inaccurate (Treiman & Kessler, 2014: Chapter 3).

Knowledge represented with explicit external symbols, such as the symbols of spoken and written language, the symbols of mathematics and logic, or the symbols of graphs and maps, differs from core cognition in many respects. It differs in format, i.e. the explicit symbol systems themselves, it most often is not innate, and it does not remain constant over development. Core cognition is mapped to the explicit symbol systems of natural language, and subsequent developments in mathematics further expand the expressive power of number representation through the mastery of culturally constructed explicit representations.

Explicit knowledge plays several unique roles in

mental life: representing causal and explanatory knowledge; supporting inferences and predictions; providing the current best guess concerning the essential properties of kinds, which play a privileged role in categorisation decisions; and on some views of conceptual content, determining those aspects of the conceptual role that separates meaning from belief (Carey, 2009: Chapter 10). These types of representations have been constructed socially, culturally and educationally throughout one's life.

6.2. Acquisition of concepts

All children arrive in the world sensitive to different kinds of perceptual experience and with an orientation to act on and make sense of their surroundings. There is wide variation in the characteristics that individual children, including those with visual impairment, bring to learning encounters (Webster & Roe, 1998: Chapter 3).

Cognitive and linguistic development can be explained systematically as follows: When we ask whether the language at one point in time (L1) and the conceptual system it expresses (CS1) might sometimes be incommensurable with the later language

(L2) and conceptual system that represents (CS2) overlapping phenomena, we are asking whether there is a set of concepts at the core of CS1 that cannot be expressed in terms of CS2, and vice versa. We are asking whether L1 can be translated into L2 without a translator's gloss. Incommensurability arises when there are simultaneous additions, deletions, differentiations, coalescences, and changes in type and core between CS1 and CS2, such that the undifferentiated concepts of CS1 no longer play a role in CS2. In cases of incommensurability, CS1 will lead to unresolvable contradictions easily resolved in CS2, and holders of CS1 will say and do things that make perfect sense from the point of CS1 that are utterly inexplicable to holders of CS2 (Carey, 2009: 376).

Children with visual impairment can build concepts that are just as elaborate as a sighted person's visualisations, but this will inevitably be a longer and less direct process. Many of the child's discoveries about the physical and logical properties of the world do not take place in isolation, but in social encounters with familiar adults; this also makes more demands of caregivers and other interactive partners. In many respects, adults will be instrumental in making bridges between the child's inner world and the world outside, with language as the medium through which this is brought about.

6.2.1. Overview of cognitive development of the blind

As Warren (1994) suggests, there is variation within the population of people with visual impairment. He believes that a truly useful body of research-based knowledge about this population must focus not on the norm or the usual but on the unusual. Their development is unusually advanced and unusually delayed because of visual impairment. We should focus on the factors in their experience that have caused their development to vary in a positive or negative direction.

The evidence clearly shows the blind infant's ability to perceive and discriminate sound stimuli. There is no evidence to controvert the thesis that perceptual discriminative capacities exist at birth and that they develop gradually over the first year in a way that is not different from the development of the sighted infant. There is nothing in the evidence about basic auditory functioning that should lead us to expect any difficulty in the development of basic auditory abilities in the blind infant or in the development of other abilities that depend on auditory perception (Warren, 1994:

17).

Importantly, tactual perceptual capacities of the blind infant are intact and develop without problem. The blind infant learns the significance of the parent's touch very early. Tactual development should serve the acquisition of other behaviours that may depend on tactile sensitivity. There is clearly a great deal of flexibility possible and a variety of scanning strategies consistently used are useful. There is an enduring belief, sometimes referred to as sensory compensation, that blindness is accompanied by an improvement in the basic acuity of the other senses, particularly hearing and touch. However, there is no consistent pattern to the occasional differences and no preponderance of evidence supports either the notion of sensory compensation or the alternative. Some researchers hypothesise that better developed habits of attention and sensitivity to stimulus are the main reason for the advantages.

For reaching outward for external stimuli, there are some indications that blind infants may lag normatively behind sighted infants, but patterns of environmental circumstances may elicit reaching earlier in some cases. In general blind infants are slower to crawl and walk than sighted infants. It is clear from evidence that lack of vision does not necessarily create a handicap, although total blindness creates a higher risk than partial vision. Muscular readiness is a prerequisite for locomotion, but it is more related to opportunity than to visual loss. Crucially, restriction of opportunity causes developmental delays in locomotion. Children with visual impairment are at risk for poor fitness, but poor fitness is not necessarily a consequence of visual impairment. The opportunities that the child has for engaging in physical activities and the encouragement that they receive to do so are the keys. Effective locomotor skills cannot develop optimally without ample opportunity and encouragement to engage that opportunity.

Children with some visual function are at an advantage in cognitive development. Furthermore, a stimulating learning environment facilitates the acquisition of cognitive abilities. This includes the nature of the curriculum and the child's participation in it, the use of out-of-school time, and the expectations held for the child's cognitive growth and educational progress. Training programmes that focus on the acquisition of concepts are an obvious manipulation of the environment, and some success has been demonstrated with them. Visual impairment may interfere with the development of allocentric spatial concepts and behaviour, and this interference should be revealed more in far space than in near space tasks.

At the same time, factors related to the child's visual history as well as other individual differences may play a significant part. Performance on tasks involving concepts of extended space varies a great deal. There is clear evidence that a period of early vision and residual visual function both facilitate performance, and intelligence is also apparently a factor. The process of acquisition of concepts of extended space is unclear, as concepts are acquired as a result of everyday experience. Early and complete visual loss does not unalterably dictate that special concepts and behaviours must be poor. These children have escaped the limitations of the attentional and information processing strategies that normally accompany blindness from birth and have adopted strategies conductive to the development of external special relationships.

The issue of word meaning is complex. Several studies on the meanings of individual words and word usage have shown that the word meanings of children with visual impairment are very similar to those of children with vision. The differences that do occur appear to be linked to the child's perceptual experiences and specifically the role of visual experience, but there is little evidence from these studies that the underlying concepts that words represent are impaired in any significant way.

Researchers have noted the tendency of blind children to use words for which they could not have had first-hand sensory experience, such as red, twinkling, or see, called verbalisms, and the interrelationships among words and their underlying concepts may be less elaborated for children with visual impairment. The use of visually based terms by the blind is not necessarily meaningless.

Children with visual impairment can experience developmental difficulties in the acquisition of referential vocabulary, such as personal pronouns and spatial-related terms. The acquisition of classification abilities in children with visual impairment generally proceeds along a normal developmental path. Variations are evident as a function of visual experience, intelligence and the child's range of experience with materials. Thus, training of classification skills may be successful, and the relationships among the skills to be trained, the training materials, and the individual child's general level of accomplishment deserve careful study.

Studies on the nature of encoding of tactual experience that show adverse effects of tactual distractors during a delay before recall suggest that tactually experienced information is encoded in a specifically tactual form. Children with early visual experience encode tactual information in a different way that is somehow affected by that experience. The better search strategies facilitate the representation of the stimulus of memory, with attention as the mediating process. As attention is more organised, so is search, the result being more effective encoding of tactually perceived information. More systematic strategies lead to better performance and strategies can benefit from training. The processing of even non-visual information about spatial structure is hampered by impaired vision.

However, strategies tend to be selected based on the particular sensory modality through which information is received. Training designed to help children to select appropriate strategies of information processing may prove useful. The evidence about tactual and phonological encoding supports the view that when stimuli have both tactual and phonological properties, these are both encoded. These processes operate interdependently, including the encoding of Braille. Children do not operate with a limitless reservoir of attention but allocate attention variously to tactual, phonological and semantic features of letters and words. In the case of tactually perceived pictorial stimuli, there are clear effects of related verbal information, and the reciprocal influence occurs.

There is no doubt that imagery facilitates verbal learning. Some results support the notion of modality-specific imagery and specifically that visual imagery is not facilitative of learning by children with visual impairment while auditory imagery is. Performance varies as a function of the imagery characteristics of the stimulus words. Blind children's performance using words with visual imagery characteristics is not facilitated, whereas auditory imagery characteristics are facilitative. Many blind children as well as adults understand what it means to represent a scene pictorially. Whether this ability is innate or learned is unclear, because there is evidence on both sides of the issue. With any set of drawings by the blind, one can see elements of configuration and of detail that are impressively mature and creative.

It is important to note that large individual differences exist among blind children's development. In general, those children who show delays in other areas of their development also present dramatically slow motor and cognitive development. Blind children who do not have a general delay still show remarkable delays in various aspects of their motor development, particularly in the acquisition of gross motor skills related to dynamic balance and self-initiated movements. During the first months of life, the exploration of the environment is based on the information coming from the use of senses and their coordination, as well as from children's actions. Blind children are at a disadvantage as compared to sighted children who can perceive external reality and the results of their actions on it in a more complete way. For the concept of object to develop, a great deal of touch exploration is needed. Touch exploration requires a slow process of development to become useful and offer reliable information on objects.

Since blind children achieve a certain level of language development, they can use language as an extremely important tool to gather information about the external world. Language and communication with others compensate blind children's lack of visual information, which results in adult proficiency in a number of cognitive domains (Perez-Pereira & Conti-Ramsden,

1999: Chapter 2).

The following list represents a continuum from concrete to abstract for developing concepts related to extending the frame of reference for blind children with the most concrete listed first. It also represents a scale of desirability of tactual experience. The more real and accurate the experience, the better (Harley, et al., 1997: 26).

Table 6-3. Concepts and blind children

- The child's own body, including self-concepts and body concepts
- The real object
- An accurate, full-scale representation of the object
- An accurate, proportionate scale model
- Stylised three-dimensional representation
- Two-dimensional representation
- Symbolic representation
- Analogical representation
- Verbal description (oral-aural inactive)
- Verbal description (oral, one way)

6.2.2. Overview of linguistic development of the blind

All the words we know and the language we speak

and eventually read and write have underlying concepts. Language development is dependent on a child's concept development, and listening plays a key role in this process.

As a child imitates and repeats words that are paired with people, objects, places and feelings, the deliberate and repetitive combination of hearing the word and at the same time touching the person or object, feeling the emotion or sensation, or being in the place helps to cement the idea or concept of the person, object, location or feeling into place. Many concepts that develop meaning within natural daily routines are easy to reinforce because they allow the child the full contextual experience that makes the concepts real. The combination of auditory and tactile stimuli that reinforce each other, paired with loving communication, provides the child with the reason to listen (Barclay, 2012: Chapter 2).

As children gain skills that help them listen, move, touch and explore, they learn more about the world through home and school routines and are introduced to more and more information. Concepts and mental images are formed as they learn to organise, recall and apply this information to new situations and in new ways. Concepts provide the information for all learning and give meaning to the language that a child learns, speaks, reads and writes. The combination of experience paired with sound and description builds concepts. Listening is an essential component and it is a powerful ingredient in concept formation when paired with touch (Barclay, 2012: Chapter 3).

The development of meaningful receptive and expressive language in children who are visually impaired may require more time than with seeing children. If there are few experiences, they may lack many of the concepts needed to develop meaningful language.

There are two different points of view on blind infants' early social and communication development. The first suggests that blind children have severe deficits in social interaction and early communication, which are similar to those presented by children with autism. Blind infants and their caregivers are not able to easily establish face-to-face and pointing interactive routines, which makes it difficult to experience the regularity and turn-taking nature of social communicative behaviours. The second argues that blind children and their parents develop alternative forms of social interaction and early communication, which are able to provide different routes for the development of the child as a social communicative being. Researchers emphasise the crucial compensatory role that language plays in blind children's development, and argue that blind infants begin to understand persons as intentional agents through learning and use of linguistic symbols (Perez-Pereira & Conti-Ramsden, 1999: Chapter 3).

According to Dunlea (1989), like sighted children, blind children begin to acquire stable vocal forms around the time of their first birthday, and have acquired 100 or more words before they are two years old. The content of early vocabularies in terms of the kinds of words used appears to be similar for blind and sighted children. However, no words acquired by blind children are dropped from their lexicons, whereas sighted children often discard terms that no longer serve their needs.

In addition, there are no idiosyncratic or created forms in blind children's lexicons. In particular, blind children's words are tied to their original context for a protracted period of time and there is little evidence of decentration. Blind children's use of words for actions and their functional or relational words describe their own activities or satisfy their own needs. They do not refer to the activities of others or encode information about the dynamic states of entities. There is no common pattern of development available and it is difficult to find clear and consistent differences with sighted children. Individual variation rather than a specific effect of vision appears to account for the differences between children.

When blind children have learned around 100 lexical items, combinations of terms are observed. Most roles emerge in requests rather than assertions. This adaptive strategy increases blind children's access to the environment. At the same time, as words are rigid, blind children begin encoding more information about themselves by combining these rigid forms. Greater contextual freedom is observed when blind children begin talking about shared past events.

Blind children need a longer period of time experiencing the world to be able to extend words to other referents of the same sort and to be able to talk more frequently about the actions performed by other people. This does not represent a lack of capacity or a qualitative difference in ability, but a restriction derived from blind children's lack of visual information regarding surrounding objects and events. Formulaic speech (chunks) seems to fulfil several important functions for blind children. It is useful to maintain conversational interchanges and to continue the conversational topic. It also allows children to express many pragmatic functions. Chunking is a useful strategy that children adopt to analyse language, particularly those phrases that are at first unanalysed sequences of sounds.

Because blind children lack visual information accompanying the speech they hear, it might be reasonable to suppose that they pay more attention to the purely auditory stimuli coming from the speech they hear. Blind children's abilities to perceive speech may well be more developed than those of sighted children. Blind children have more difficulties in discriminating and producing those sounds that have visually perceptible articulation. The results suggest that blind children may be slightly delayed in learning those sounds that have clear visual articulation, but older blind children show normal use of speech sounds. Blind children in due course can make use of acoustic information to correct their substitutions and to achieve standard adult pronunciation. Research with deaf children has shown that vision alone may not be of much help in developing articulation skills: auditory input is crucial for articulatory development.

Table 6-4. Possibly affected aspects of development

Preverbal communication	Smiling; gesture; eye gaze; reciprocal vocalisation; mutual focus of attention; nonverbal interaction; pointing and reaching
Speech sounds	Extended babbling period; perception of speech sounds; articulation of the full range of speech sounds through not necessarily disordered phonology
Early language	Age of onset and rate of development; lexical structure; morphology; syntax
Use of language	Use of language without full understanding; understanding sighted words; terms for spatial relations; personal pronouns

(Bozic & Murdoch, eds., 1996: 117)

Regarding verbalism, it has been argued that other sources of meaning exist, apart from the sensorial or experiential ones, such as the word-to-word or intralinguistic relationships in the semantic structure of the language, or the structural sources of meaning. The position that blind children have different meanings for words than their sighted counterparts and live in a meaningless world seems to be untenable.

One of the most striking studies is Landau & Gleitman's research (1985) on the acquisition of visual and colour terms by a congenitally blind child. Blind children have meanings similar to those of sighted children, even if it is likely that blind children take a longer time to construct conceptual meanings of some words. In addition to direct experience of the external world, blind children may rely on the use of the information presented by language itself.

The analysis of more specifically syntactic aspects of language indicates that lack of vision itself does not cause delay. There is general agreement that morphosyntactic development is not delayed in blind children. The emergence and percentage of use of coordinate and subordinate clauses show that blind children follow a normal pattern of development as compared with sighted children. As blind children mature, they seem to acquire and use the full breadth of lexical items available in language as part of becoming effective communicators. Blind children are certain to be placed in general education settings these days, since their sensory impairment should not have an effect on language and communication use in school learning. Interacting with and assisting children with visual impairment to experience full access to communication and learning is certain to be one of the most rewarding activities (Damico, et al., eds., 2010: Chapter

3).

One of the defining characteristics of human language is arbitrariness: there is no logical or natural relationship between the word and its meaning. The association is a mere convention and we must learn each word on its own.

However, some vocabulary words in human languages are not so arbitrary: we can intuitively perceive some correspondences between sound and meaning. The vocabulary words created as a result of such experience are called ideophones. Japanese is well known for its rich inventory of ideophones. The clearest ideophone subtype is onomatopoeia, which mimic actual sounds. Moreover, such a direct correspondence between sound and meaning is occasionally extended to visual, glossal (taste), tactile (touching) and other kinds of sensations and impressions (Hasegawa, 2015: 71).

Blind individuals make use of such expressions fairly frequently and naturally as normal sighted people do. Like their proper use of colour terms, they develop a semantic network surrounding a noun and a verb as a phrase.

6.3. Input systems and language processing

The majority of books on human perception consider each of the senses, e.g. vision, hearing, olfaction, and taste, in isolation as if each one represented an entirely separate and independent perceptual system (Bacci & Melcher, eds., 2013: Chapter 4). In fact, wherever one looks, the standard approach is to look at the role and influence of each sense in isolation with rarely any thought given to how the senses may interact with one another. In many situations, our senses receive correlated information about the same external objects and events. This information is typically combined to yield the multisensorially determined sensations that fill our daily lives.

It is worth bearing in mind that humans can interface with language as a cognitive system using sounds, sign and text (visual) as well as Braille (tactile). The system can connect with input/output processes in any sensory modality. Language processing consists of a complex and nested set of subroutines to get from sound to meaning or meaning to sound with remarkable speed and accuracy.

6.3.1. Auditory, visual and tactile sensations

When listening to speech, the first requirement is that the continuous speech input is perceptually segmented into discrete entities that can be mapped onto and will activate abstract phonological representations that are stored in long-term memory. This word recognition process happens extremely fast and is completed within a few hundred milliseconds. Given the rate of typical speech (4 – 7 syllables per second), we can deduce that word recognition is extremely efficient, taking no more than 200 – 300 milliseconds.

Recognising word forms is an entrance point for the retrieval of syntactic (lemma) and semantic (conceptual) information. In most cases, the phrase structure context generates strong predictions about the syntactic slot that will be filled by the current lexical item. Most of the retrieval and integration processes are completed within 500 milliseconds.

The cognitive architecture necessary to realise language is tripartite in nature, with form (speech sounds, graphemes including letters and Braille in text, or manual gestures in sign language), syntactic structure, and meaning as the core components of our language faculty. These three levels are domain-specific, but they interact during incremental language processing.

Spatial structures have been considered as though they are some sort of souped-up visual images, but we can use our sense of touch to determine the shapes and arrangements of objects. The sense of shape we get haptically has to line up somehow with the sense of shape we get visually. The sensation of taking in a shape with our eyes might be totally different from the sensation of taking in a shape by moving our hand across it, but these two sensations add up to the same understanding. The congenitally blind ought to have a pretty good understanding of shape and spatial layout for things they can reach and touch (Jackendoff, 2012: Chapter 24; Sharwood Smith & Truscott, 2014).

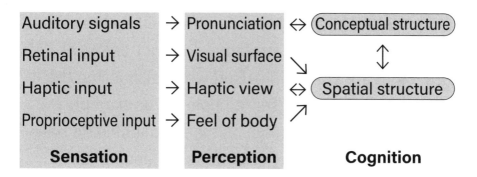

Sensation	Sensation generally refers to physical stimulation at the organs of sense, or the neural signals we receive from the sense organs.
Perception	Perception implies a conscious awareness of the information that comes through sensation. The process of perception of a sensory stimulus involves sensation, memory and motivation.
Cognition	Cognition is a generic term that is broadly concerned with the mental processes by which we acquire, organise and use knowledge as we come to know and understand the world. It involves different levels of mental processing, including problem solving, memory, attention and perception.

Some readers might be a bit puzzled by the differences in terminology. To clarify, succinct definitions of terms that are commonly used when discussing the sense of touch are presented below. For example, although the terms haptic, tactual, and tactile do have distinct meanings, they are frequently used interchangeably (McLinden & McCall, 2002: Appendix).

Haptic	Haptic means 'able to touch'. As an adjective, the term can be used as relating to the sense of touch and is usually combined with the term perception. Haptic perception refers to perception that relates to the sense of touch. More particularly, it concerns the recognition of sensory information that is received through the manipulation and exploration of the object's properties, e.g. size, shape, weight and texture. The term is sometimes described as active touch.
Tactile	Tactile is commonly used to describe the qualities or properties of objects that are accessible through the sense of touch. Tactile refers to the physical features or properties of an object that can be detected through the sense of touch, e.g. its contours, surface temperature and/or weight.
Tactual	Tactual has a similar derivation to the term tactile and is frequently used interchangeably in the literature with both tactile and haptic to refer to the sense of touch. Tactual refers to the exploratory and manipulative actions we perform on objects and sensory features to acquire information about these properties.

A large body of experimental data has now convincingly shown that the haptic perception of both the structural and surface properties of objects as well as their perceived functionality can be profoundly influenced by what people see, what they hear and what they smell. In terms of the precise weighting of the input from each of the senses to our overall tactile experience, the evidence now supports the view that each and every sense that is stimulated can contribute to our overall multisensory perceptual experience.

6.3.2. Formulaic sequences for accurate and fluent processing

Formulaic sequences refer to sequences of words that are in some regard not entirely predictable, whether on account of a meaning that is widely or subtly different from the words they contain, a function that is only achieved with the whole expression, or features of structure, such as morphology or word order, that are non-canonical. In other words, a formulaic sequence is a continuous or discontinuous sequence of words or other meaning elements that appears to be prefabricated. They are stored and retrieved whole from memory at the time of use as one chunk, rather than being subject to generation or analysis by the language grammar (Wray, 2002).

Speech formulas play an important role in first and second language acquisition. It is now clear that learners reuse sequences of words taken directly and seemingly unanalysed from the input. Such formulaic sequences are central to language development. This occurs at all levels of the language system, which emerges from the statistical abstraction of patterns latent within and across form and function in language use. Language processing is sensitive to the sequential probabilities of linguistic elements at all levels from phonemes to phrases in comprehension as well as in fluency and idiomaticity of speech production. There has been considerable recent research investigating learners' sensitivity to formulaic sequences both in fluent comprehension and production (ARAL, 2012; Nakamori, 2009; Wood, 2010; Wray, 2002, 2008).

Recent scientific brain research has shown that the brain represents formulaic sequences in long-term memory, bypassing the need to compose them online through word selection and grammatical sequencing in capacity-limited working memory. There is an advantage in the way that native speakers process formulaic language compared to non-formulaic language. This advantage extends to the access and use of different types of formulaic language, including binominals, collocations, idioms, and lexical bundles. Formulaic sequences are stored as a whole and they are accessed rapidly for accurate, fluent, and natural use in communication (ARAL, 2012: 45; Wood, 2012).

6.3.3. Frequency effects in language learning and processing

From its very beginnings, psychological research has recognised three major experimental factors that affect cognition: frequency, recency, and context. Learning, memory, and perception are all affected by frequency of usage: the more times we experience something, the stronger our memory for it, and the more fluently it is accessed. The more recently we have experienced something, the stronger our memory for it, and the more fluently it is accessed. The more times we recognise features, the more they become associated in our minds and the more these subsequently affect perception and categorisation; so a stimulus becomes associated to a context and we become more likely to perceive it in that context (Gries & Divjak, eds., 2012: 7; Sedlmeier & Betsch, 2002).

Let us consider what is meant by 'fluency'. Fluency experiences are common but people do not always focus on them. Although people are familiar with fluency experiences, what exactly fluency is as a scientific concept may still be blurry. Unkelbach & Greifeneder (2013: 3) list five core components of fluency.

Table 6-5. Components of fluency

Fluency is a feeling: It provides experiential information about otherwise inaccessible mental processes and thus feedback about the state of the cognitive system.
Fluency arises as a by-product from mental operations: It has been characterised as the experiential output of an internal monitoring system that constantly screens how mental processing proceeds.
Fluency is informative about the ease or difficulty with which some mental operation is executed.
The subjective location of a specific experience on the easy-difficult dimension is a function of prior experiences.
Fluency is an integrative experience that summarises ongoing mental activity.

Processing fluency is the ease with which a stimulus is processed. Subjective processing fluency denotes the phenomenal feeling of ease of processing, whereas objective processing fluency denotes the underlying objective speed of processing. The speeds of processing at different stages contribute jointly to the phenomenal experience of processing fluency. Feelings may provide contextual information in a highly condensed form. In other words, the phenomenal experience of processing fluency may provide highly condensed information about the simplicity, frequency and familiarity of a stimulus, or about the potential effort connected to stimulus elaboration (Sedlmeier & Betsch, 2002: Chapter 11).

In the process of language acquisition, a child moves from an initial state of limited language comprehension and production to a state of adult-like language use. During this process, innate structures and their interaction with the input are assigned a different status by the two leading approaches in linguistics (Gulzow & Gagarina, eds., 2007: Introduction).

For theories that assume the existence of a rich inventory of innate structures, the question of how frequency of exposure leads to acquisition is basically irrelevant. Theoretically, single exposure may be as successful as many, or when arguments of an impoverished stimulus are considered, even in cases in which exposure is absent or ambiguous, acquisition is believed to take place.

Frequency-based models of language learning claim that linguistic knowledge is mainly shaped by linguistic experience: frequency of events in input largely determines how linguistic knowledge is represented and processed in the mind. These models suggest that humans are able to detect frequencies of events that they perceive and experience implicitly, and information concerning the frequencies is stored mentally, affecting how the perceived events are processed and organised.

Experimental studies have shown that higher frequency phrases are processed faster across the frequency range (Divjak & Gries, eds., 2012). The more often a phrase had been experienced, the faster and more fluently it was processed. Language users are sensitive to the frequency of common word combinations, just as they are to the frequency of single words. However, formulaic sequences, including idiomatic phrases, are not unanalysed wholes but have internal structure when they are stored. This means that a learner eventually gets to know the sound sequence /hauzitgouin/ is spelt out as 'How's it going'. To enhance this process, consciousness raising, awareness and attention, noticing, and focus on form have been proposed in learning environments where learners are likely to memorise sound sequences as a whole and communicate by using them without realising from what words such chunks consist of.

As elements with a high frequency may nevertheless appear relatively late in acquisition while there are non-frequent elements that are acquired early, distribution cannot be regarded as being equally relevant in all cases. It is a well-known fact that the distribution of linguistic elements in the input, such as articles and pre/postpositions, is mirrored from early on or remains absent for a relatively long time in the process of first language acquisition.

Moreover, it is extremely difficult for foreign language learners to attain proficiency of these elements at the same level as native speakers of the language, which suggests that frequencies would not help in some cases because articles are one of the most frequent elements in language. It is too simplistic and unrealistic to claim that frequent exposure to language solves all learning problems that learners may encounter. For instance, definite and indefinite articles, number-, case- and gender-agreements, tense marking, and pre/postpositions are very frequent, but adult learners often make mistakes with them. Adult learners do not possess automatic unconscious processing of these features (Nakamori, 2009: Chapter 2).

Chapter 7

Phonological chunking and foreign language learning

Introduction

Sound has the potential to entice, educate, and entertain us. In our daily lives, listening and speaking skills are fundamental to all types of social interaction, intrinsic to many leisure activities, necessary for most types of work, and essential to all aspects of education. Given how important they are, these skills are taken for granted. We do not usually think about how we communicate since it is as instinctive as walking (Lancaster, 2008: 13).

Listening and speaking skills are particularly important to people with visual impairment, as the world is not full of accessible text in some situations. It may be more appropriate for them to listen rather than read or to speak rather than write in many occasions.

To attain linguistic proficiency, blind learners must

depend primarily on acoustic imitation since they cannot observe the muscular movements that accompany articulation. They are more influenced by acoustic similarity of sounds, whereas sighted learners' sound substitutions may also involve visual similarities in the way sounds are made.

This chapter discusses the implications for foreign language learning and teaching communicative skills to visually impaired students.

7.1. Principles of teaching

Perception and production of a foreign language often involve learning difficulties. Numerous studies have revealed that perception tends to be more accurate than production in a foreign language.

However, there are many reports that indicate that learners are able to produce sounds of a foreign language that they have difficulty perceiving correctly. For instance, Japanese learners of English are better able to differentiate /r/ and /l/ in production than in perception. This is because these learners pay close attention to the way they are articulating themselves when producing the sounds. They have been taught the place and manner of articulation with pictures of a mouth when practising pronunciation. It is now clear that perception and production employ different systems in the brain, that they develop on their own, and that they influence each other, as we saw in Section 3.2.

Planning for learning is helped if teachers are able to consider how students learn and a useful model of learning that incorporates all aspects of communication (Godwin & Perkins, 2002: Chapter 1):

1. **Engagement**: setting the scene. Intention to learn arises when learners become curious or puzzled about what they are to learn. What they must learn must matter to them as well as to their teacher.
2. **Exploration** allows learners to become involved in the learning process by relating new information to their past experiences.
3. **Transformation** is a play stage where new information is reshaped and worked with so that the learner can move closer to further understanding.
4. **Presentation strategies**, whereby learners explain their developing understanding to others, play a significant part in the process of assimilating new information.

5. **Reflection** on what and how they have learned is an important part in accommodating new information to what they already know.

According to Best (1992), there are a number of general factors that need to be considered when devising an appropriate teaching style for use with any learner with visual impairment.

7.1.1. Position

The learner's work position needs to be considered. There may need to be access to electric sockets in order to use a desk lamp, a CD/tape recorder, a computer or other equipment. The learner will need an appropriate level of glare-free lighting on the work surface. Height and angle of tables and chairs must be considered as well. There needs to be smooth access to stored equipment. A learner will be helped by having the opportunity to explore the classroom areas in the absence of other people and to practise moving through routes with some guidance.

7.1.2. Presentation

Visual difficulties can particularly affect access to print, and the way this material is presented greatly influences the ease, accuracy and speed of working for a learner. Size and colour of letters as well as their arrangements should be carefully adjusted.

Presentations of information in a written form need to be supplemented with spoken information. This is a quicker way of getting information and the use of recorders is recommended. It is necessary for teachers to add verbal explanations and descriptions of what they are writing or doing in order to enable a learner with visual impairment to follow a lesson. The presentation of material in tactile form needs special consideration. Giving concrete information tactually is particularly important when working with blind learners.

7.1.3. Experience

Learners with visual impairments need access to first-hand experience whenever possible. They should not have to rely solely on descriptions given by other people of situations they cannot see clearly. These descriptions will not be as full or meaningful as a first-hand experience, will place additional demands on the learner's memory, or will appear to reduce the worth of the learner's own perceptions and experiences, removing some of the active involvement in learning through discovering. Learners with visual impairment will almost certainly have reduced access to experiences that other learners have.

7.1.4. Expectations

In general, it is probably wise to require the same standard of behaviour from a learner with visual impairment as expected from other learners, while accepting that the learner's speed of working will be slower than that of a normal-sighted person. A great deal of concentration is required for many activities, which makes them hard and tiring.

Reading Braille one character at a time, or learning through listening without being able to watch the speaker's face, require considerably more concentration than reading or listening with perfect vision. So it would not be surprising if a learner had a lapse of concentration and missed a vital point or became frustrated when trying to understand a complex piece of work. This may be particularly the case for a learner in the process of losing his/her sight or who has recently become visually impaired.

7.1.5. Giving information

To many learners with visual impairment, a teacher's

voice will be their major source of information. It is helpful if it is pleasant and interesting to listen to, and it needs to give accurate information. A relaxed tone is much easier to listen to than a strained or tense voice. The pitch of a voice can also communicate certainty, anxiety or boredom, and these signals can be picked up more sensitively by those who are not receiving the nonverbal clues, such as facial expressions and gestures.

Selection of words for accurate information is also critical. Daily usage by sighted people may contain many inadequacies that could be improved to help a learner not being able to see the demonstration or process clearly. Actions could be replaced by more accurate verbs, vague expressions could be replaced by appropriate nouns, and places could be elaborated to the precise location. The words will have to carry all the meaning that the teacher needs to convey, and visually dependent information ideally needs to be replaced by clearer verbal expressions. Scaffolding, paraphrasing, and appropriate linguistic feedback are important.

7.1.6. Speed

Learners may take longer to find their place in a book,

locate a piece of equipment, write a sentence, or undertake almost any activity. They may need to peer, feel, check, replace, identify, absorb, put together and integrate as part of their exploration. The non-visual learner who uses touch will certainly need extra time to understand. Being rushed in work tasks or mobility can be very frustrating or frightening.

One common folk belief is that those who lose the sense of vision develop better capacities in perceiving auditory information. Recent evidence suggests that this is indeed the case. For instance, blind individuals are better able to localise sound sources, which is obviously quite useful given that they cannot rely upon any visual cue. In addition, blind individuals are faster in processing auditory language stimuli than their sighted counterparts (Bacci & Melcher, eds., 2013: Chapter 14).

The average rate for print reading aloud is 120 wpm, but the listener can process speech at a much faster rate than it is normally delivered. With practice, listening speeds approaching or even exceeding average silent print reading rates (250 wpm) can be attained. This ability enables students in higher education to process large amounts of material effectively by ear.

Some teachers have proposed that learners need to have access to high-speed utterances by means of artificial listening training. The disadvantage of some variable speed recorders is that as the speed of the tape is accelerated, the pitch of the speaker's voice rises and the listener finds it increasingly uncomfortable to listen to. In particular, the female voice with its initial higher pitch is especially difficult for listeners to comprehend when played at higher speeds.

On the other hand, in compressed speech, the speed of reading is increased but the original pitch is restored by means of a pitch control device and the words are electronically sampled and shortened without loss of intelligibility. With this method, speech of 150 wpm can be increased to 275 wpm without affecting comprehension, although for most learners comprehension diminishes rapidly when speeds are increased above 300 wpm (Mason & McCall, eds., 1997: Chapter 15).

7.2. Listening skills

It has been widely considered that hearing is the reception of sound while listening implies paying specific attention to the sound with the express intention of interpreting its meaning. Whereas hearing is the passive ability to receive sound, listening is a deliberate process by which sound is given meaning. More precisely, hearing is the physiological process through which sound waves are collected through the ear and auditory information is transmitted to the brain. Listening, on the other hand, is the act of assigning meaning to what is heard.

Humans attach meaning to what they hear by combining their senses of vision, touch and hearing. During listening, the auditory cortex of the brain acts in tandem with other parts of the brain, integrating sensory input in order to interpret what is heard. Most people use visual cues to combine vision with sound to help them process what they are hearing. For the individual with a visual impairment who does not receive visual input for clarification, this active cognitive process that involves attaching meaning to hearing takes a unique path. It needs to be more deliberate and more experiential, that is, taught through experience providing emphasis on the pairing of language and touch, action and objects. Individuals' lack of opportunity for incidental learning, their ability to learn about the world by simply watching what goes on around them, necessitates a more conscious effort to help compensate for the visual information that is missing (Barclay, 2012: Chapter 1).

Mason & McCall (1997: Chapter 15) claim that it is a commonly held misconception that people who are blind automatically develop a better sense of hearing to compensate for their sight loss. Teachers of learners with a visual impairment are aware that listening skills do not develop naturally but need to be taught through a systematic programme of instruction.

Listening is the foundation for developing other skills. Before children become readers and writers, they need to be proficient listeners and speakers. Developing listening skills prepares children for the other modes of communication, as we reviewed in Chapter 5. This is true for foreign language learning as well. At an early stage, oral communicative interaction provides the basis for comprehension in first language acquisition and foreign language learning. Input should be presented to learners through a myriad of resources and awareness-raising activities. Focused listening tasks where learners participate actively in the listening process involve listeners not only in listening for a purpose but also in becoming active participants in the communication process (Mourao & Lourenco, eds., 2015: Chapter 9).

Sounds and words have a central position for the learner with visual impairment. To use this information efficiently requires good listening skills. In this book, 'listening' is interpreted in its broadest possible sense, including its importance for language and concept development, literacy learning, social skills, technology use, and orientation and mobility.

For instance, the whoosh of water from the faucet into the tub, the dripping of rain from a gutter, the rush of a creek under a bridge, and the crashing of waves at the beach represent just some of the sounds of water, and with repeated experiences with many aspects of water in many contexts, including opportunities to hear, touch, label and compare it in various forms, children with visual impairment can begin to learn to understand the many sounds that water can make. Similarly, they can develop listening skills and comprehension of the world that surrounds them in turn.

Learning to listen permeates every aspect of our lives. When one travels, listening to the auditory cues in the environment provides a memory map to assist with route planning and recognition of cues in the environment. In an academic environment, one learns to take in valuable information by listening to key ideas and information presented by others. Listening to the speaker, determining the most salient information to record, and recording the information in Braille or print ensures systematic organisation of information (Barclay, 2012).

Most of the literature on listening for learners who are visually impaired deals with analytical listening. The following hierarchical objectives would be appropriate for learning analytical listening skills for communication in first and second language environments (Harley, et al., 1997: 226).

Table 7-1. Listening skills for communication

1. Discriminate and identify verbal and nonverbal sounds
2. Demonstrate listener-speaker responsibility
3. Recall facts and details   4. Identify sequential order
5. Select main ideas   6. Summarise
7. Relate one idea to another   8. Make inferences
9. More advanced skills: • find emotional persuasion, make judgements   • recognise stated cause and effect relationships   • draw conclusions, make generalisations   • recognise purpose, determine accuracy of information   • differentiate fact from opinion, discount bias of speaker   • recognise propaganda techniques, find hidden purpose   • solve problems, predict outcomes

Interestingly, some recent studies have specifically investigated the role of improved auditory processing in determining superior auditory memory in the blind. Blind people outperform the sighted in standard digit span and word repletion tasks. The improved memory abilities of blind people depend on improved stimulus processing at an early stage of encoding rather than on superior abilities at subsequent memory-related processes.

Improved sensory encoding allows the sequencing and chunking that support better memory performance. Memory advantages in the blind depend on their ability to chunk together consecutively presented items. The short-term memory advantage of blind individuals results from better stimulus encoding ability (Cattaneo & Vecchi, 2011: 28). This is where the significance of phonological chunking in foreign language learning comes in.

From the earliest stages, the sound of speech will be used by learners to help identify the speaker. Later, the words themselves will be an important source of information to supplement the learner's own visual or tactile experiences. In listening to speech, a learner will have to concentrate on the words and extract meaning from the sound sequences.

We can imagine that normal-sighted people can see a person's mouth moving, interpret a facial expression that adds meaning to the words, and anticipate somebody joining in a conversation by noting his/her appearance over there, but blind learners will need to hear every word and sound clearly and understand what is said solely with this verbal information. Concentrating is easier in quiet surroundings if the speaker allows time for information to be heard and absorbed, if there is variation in the speed, pitch and volume of the speaker's voice, and if the learner is engaged in the words through the use of frequent questions.

Some students with visual impairment find they can often use an IC/tape recorder very well. They use it as a memo pad or for note taking. Basically, all learners with visual impairment need to use recorded information more or less. A high-quality recording will help considerably, and it is necessary to give careful attention to the details of the recording technique in order to provide material that is pleasant to listen to over a period of time.

To produce recorded materials or to record the learner's voice for study, the recording should be made in a place in which there will not be interference from sounds, such as passing trains, people in the corridor, cars and buses, extractor fans, telephones, and other noise makers. At certain times of the day, a location may be much freer from possible interference than at other times. One common source of sound distraction is the table surface on which the recording is made. A cloth surface of carpet or towelling is better than a noisy hard surface such as wood. The speaker should be able to speak at a reasonably constant rate with correct and fluent pronunciation, particularly if the recording is to be used at an accelerated rate.

An external microphone or a headset of high quality will enable making a clearer recording of the speech sounds. Personal computers nowadays are equipped with basic recording systems. For beginners of foreign language learning, audio speakers of good quality that produce wide ranges of frequencies are recommended, as human auditory mechanisms tune in different frequencies when learning sounds of a foreign language, as we saw in Section 1.3.1. After they become sensitive to sounds of the foreign language, learners need to get used to different sound qualities, including various accents of a wide spectrum of speakers, bad sound quality, and unclear articulation.

Table 7-2. Development of listening skills

Basic skills	• Becoming aware of the sound • Discriminating one sound from another • Identifying the source of the sound • Attaching meaning to the sound
Higher skills	• Discover the main ideas • Recognise a sequence of events • Predict outcomes • Remember details from a complicated text • Recognise stated or inferred cause and effect • Recognise pivotal words that are cues to sequence, contrast, cues and effect • Distinguish between fact and opinion • Appreciate shades of meaning expressed by various words • Make value judgements • Evaluate the source of the information • Adjust the pattern of listening and thinking to the type of material and listening purpose • Select and summarise material pertinent to the listening purpose

7.3. Phonological chunking and communication skills

Traditionally, communication research focused on the way messages were sent, i.e. the form and the content of these messages. This approach cannot fully explain the difficulties one has on a daily basis communicating with other people. In reality, researchers suggest that the following levels would need to be considered (O'Kane & Goldbart, 1998: Chapter 8):

Table 7-3. Three-level message analysis

Context	Communicative intent	Range and form
	Organisation of discourse	Turn-taking; topic initiation; maintenance and termination; breakdown and repair
	Presupposition	Informativeness; social context, including communication partner, communication channels and setting

Oracy (listening and speaking) represents the individual's ability to use a set of oral language processing and production skills in communication. Oracy roughly parallels literacy (reading and writing) as a construct

(Godwin & Perkins, 2002; Tarone, et al., 2009). The acquisition of a speech system sees the development of both speech perception and speech production processes. These processes rely on an analysis of the acoustic phonetic properties of the speech stream. The attainment of speech perception and production processes is integrally related. The development of speech perception is thought to progress along three levels.

1. **Detection**

    It is first important for the language learner to have sufficient hearing sensitivity to be able to detect incoming speech sounds. These speech sounds vary according to both their temporal and spectral structure, and the level and type of background noise against which they are presented. The consequence of this is that a variety of auditory processing abilities are required for accurate speech sound detection. For instance, hearing sensitivity at high frequencies is important for the detection of fricatives, and efficient temporal processing mechanisms are central to the detection of stop consonants. The auditory systems of humans born with normal hearing show near adult-like sensitivity across the frequency range significant for speech by six months of age.

2. **Discrimination**

   Speech discrimination refers to the processes by which listeners distinguish different speech sounds. The predominant view was that infants are born pre-programmed to perceive the phonetic boundaries of all the world's languages. However, more recent research has suggested that previous studies may have overestimated the speech discrimination skills of humans. Exposure to a language affects perceptual weight assigned to particular acoustic properties of speech. With linguistic exposure, learners gradually increase their attention towards the static properties of speech that provide information about the phonetic structure.

3. **Identification**

   Speech identification denotes the process by which we categorise spoken words into their constituent parts. The perceptual challenge for learners is to identify the smallest units of speech so that they know which sounds can be treated as variants of the same phones, and which signal distinct phones capable of altering word meaning.

This skill is known as phonological awareness.

To enrich their lexicon, learners must be able to identify both recurring phonological sequences in the speech stream and the concepts that those sequences represent, and map phonology onto word meaning. It is important for learners to have sufficient auditory information to extract a stable phonological representation of the sequence of sounds contained within the word in order to avoid the potential confusion of similar sounding words.

In addition, audition plays a key role in morphological and syntactic development. It has been suggested that syntax can be bootstrapped by prosodic cues in speech, which provide additional information about the structure and grouping of an utterance. The auditory basis of pragmatics comprises the suprasegmental phonology of the speech signal.

There is considerable evidence to support the suggestion that reading is dependent on an auditory code, as we looked at in Section 5.1. It is generally accepted that the development of word coding is heavily dependent upon phonological processing skills. Research has shown that reading problems are most commonly associated with phonological issues.

In order to extract meaning from a passage of text, readers must draw upon their knowledge of language that is involved in sound codes (Plack, ed., 2010: Chapter 15).

There are three main factors to consider in establishing the special needs of learners with visual impairment (Best, 1992):

1. Without the use of the coordinating sense of vision, exploration will be through sequential experiences that have to be synthesised into a whole. This is complex and takes more time than normal exploration.
2. The features and characteristics that are of help and interest to a learner exploring tactually may be different from those that are important to the sighted learner.
3. The quantity and quality of experiences will be restricted and this will make incidental learning difficult.

One of the roles of educators is to help their learners overcome these effects of visual handicap by enabling them to gain access to the experiences they need. They will need more accurate and structured information tactually as well as verbally and more time to assimilate information. The following listening skills for communication should be developed at the intermediate and advanced levels:

Table 7-4. Attaining listening skills for communication

Listen for factual details
This may be practised through setting questions about facts in the passage that the learner should listen for.
Selective listening
Activities can be given to a learner or a group of learners in which they have to pick out certain sounds from amongst other distracting background noises or identify out of place phrases in a passage.
Informative listening
This requires a learner to identify the main or topic sentence in a passage.
Evaluative listening
The learner should identify if opinions or facts are being expressed and may go on to separate statements from supporting evidence.

To summarise, the following factors influence perception of speakers. Crucial elements include pitch changes, loudness, temporal cues and voice quality (Kreiman & Sidtis, 2011: Chapters 7 & 8):

1. Inherent ability to remember and recognise voices
2. Degree of attention
3. Confidence in memorising what is heard
4. Sex of listener
5. Effects of training
6. Accuracy of description of what is heard

One way in which new vocabulary and expressions are learned is in the form of what are referred to as formulaic sequences, as discussed in Section 6.3.2. Learners appear to learn them as single unanalysed units or ready-made chunks. These appear to serve as building blocks in foreign language learning. These units may serve to simplify the complex learning task, since a single unit can be used to express a complex thought or idea.

In communication, learners tend to use formulaic language that contains language structures that are beyond their current level of mastery. By using formulaic language, learners ease somewhat the language learning task. Formulaic language lightens the attentional and processing burdens of utterance construction and enables fast and fluid communication (Wood, 2010).

Increased facility with formulaic language enhances fluency in a foreign language. By learning formulaic sequences, more processing resources can be devoted to focusing on other linguistic aspects of the target language. As we saw in the previous section, visually impaired learners tend to attain longer chunks, which help them communicate.

To use English naturally, it is important to be aware of combinations of words. It is often useful to start with a noun and notice the adjectives, verbs and other nouns that they collocate with. In addition, we should pay attention to grammatical features of them, including whether the noun is singular or plural and whether it goes with 'a', 'the' or no article.

Restrictions on the combination of words are referred to as collocations, which are sequences of words that function like a single lexical item. According to Sinclair (1987), the definition of regular or significant collocates is lexical items occurring within five words either way of the headword with a greater frequency than the law of averages would lead you to expect. Collocations are related to fixed expressions, formulaic sequences, idioms, lexical (set) phrases, and so on.

Collocations are statistically determined clusters or relatively fixed chunks. The collection of lexical items that commonly co-occur before or after a given word often forms a cluster. Sometimes, collocations obey inherent semantic and syntactic patterns of particular lexical items, which are categorised by the extent to which they form fixed units called chunks.

By adopting the Lexical Approach, Nakamori (2009) emphasised the learning of formulaic language and of phonological chunking processes in the language classroom. Activities that raise awareness of the lexical nature of language can aid learning. It is important to pay attention to the natural ways of pronunciation as well as their components; otherwise, learners do not understand the exact words that consist of the formulaic language. For instance, learners may hear and use the phrase /hauzitgouin/ in daily conversation, but they may not know how this sequence is spelt out.

Blind students often repeat and use formulaic language fluently without noticing the words in it, because visual information, such as written materials, is limited. After practising formulaic sequences, each word in them needs to be told orally or provided by Braille.

As we saw in Section 6.3.2, a growing body of work suggests that ready-made chunks or preferred sequences of words play a significant part in language acquisition and processing. These formulaic language sequences are multiword units of language that are stored in long-term memory as if they were single lexical units.

Common chunks are as follows:

Situational formulas	These fit into certain conversational parameters, e.g. *how are you, excuse me.*
Stylistic formulas	These are specific to particular registers of language, e.g. *in conclusion, by way of conclusion.*
Ceremonial formulas	These are ritualistic and required by certain formal settings, e.g. *ladies and gentlemen, may I have your attention please.*
Gambits	These organise interactions or activities, e.g. *what do you think, it's your turn.*

Accuracy and fluency can be facilitated by attention to formulaic language, and an assortment of activities that incorporate this exists already in materials and course designs, but much more work needs to be done on building processing-based courses and integrating knowledge about language processing into all elements of language teaching programmes (Wood, 2010).

Based on our discussions of this book, in particular those in Sections 3.4 and 4.4, the following speech learning programme with a personal computer can be recommended. We should be aware of the fact that we hear sounds through both our bones (bone-conducted) and our eardrums (air-conducted). Most sounds are heard by our eardrums, which convert the sound waves to vibrations and transmits them to the cochlea. However, vibrations are heard directly in some cases by the inner ear, bypassing our eardrums. In fact, this is one of the ways we hear our own voice. If we hear our recorded voice, we are puzzled because we feel the recorded speech is spoken by a different person from us. As we hear ourselves by bone conduction, the sound quality is not the same as the recording. People, excluding ourselves, hear our voices by air conduction only.

Table 7-5. Attaining speaking skills for communication

Principles:

1. The following procedure consists of one cycle, and the amount of practice of repeating it depends on how well the learner masters the sequence of sounds.
2. It is important for the learner to lengthen the sequence gradually from words to phrases to a sentence, because he/she needs to adjust his/her articulators, such as the tongue, lips, and jaw.
3. The learner is expected to optimise his/her articulation so that the effect of the practice carries over to new contexts and situations. He/she has to focus on grammar and meaning, so it will be hard to monitor articulations.

Age range	Training programme
By age 9	Children can imitate/mimic everything they hear, so disordered speech or strong accents, including foreign accents of non-native teachers, should be avoided. Voices of kids and adults can be used.
	Speak into a microphone → Listen to the model pronunciation → Speak into a microphone → Listen to the model pronunciation

From ages 10 to 15	Adolescents can notice/recognise the differences in sounds between theirs and the model. Low-frequency voices of adult males and females sound prescriptive for them.
	Speak into a microphone → Listen to their recorded pronunciation → Speak into a microphone → Listen to the model pronunciation → Speak into a microphone → Listen to their recorded pronunciation → Listen to the model pronuncation
Over age 16	Adults feel more comfortable if they understand why their pronunciations sound different from the model. Figures and animations that point out improvements would help. They like to hear voices of their age group.
	Speak into a microphone → Listen to their recorded pronunciation → Speak into a microphone → Listen to the model pronunciation and understand the differences and the points to improve → Speak into a microphone → Listen to their recorded pronunciation → Listen to the model pronunciation

7.4. Tactile skills

The sense of touch produces a number of distinct sensory experiences. Each type of experience is mediated by its own sensory receptor systems. Tactile receptors are responsive not only to pressure but to vibration, changes in temperature, and noxious stimulation. The kinaesthetic system, which contributes to our sense of touch, is involved in sensing limb position and the movement of our limbs in space. The sense of touch is intimately related to our ability to perform actions.

Touch is better adapted to feeling the material properties of objects than it is to feeling their geometric features, such as shape, particularly when an object is large enough to extend beyond the fingertip.

For instance, in the Braille alphabet, each letter is formed by raising some of the dots in a 2 × 3 array. This design reflects a compromise between the skin's acuity and its field of view, the area of skin that we can take in all at once. It would be nice to include more than six dots in the array, but because of the spatial blurring imposed by the skin, denser patterns would be difficult to resolve and discriminate as two-point thresholds on the fingertips are about 1mm. Spreading a greater number of dots across a larger contact area would not work either, because the pattern would extend beyond the fingertip. Unfortunately, people are unable to read more than one finger at a time, suggesting that our tactile field of view is very narrow (Wolfe, et al., 2012: Chapter 13).

Like other sensory modalities, touch gives rise to internal representations of the world, which convey the positions of objects using the body as a spatial reference system. Touch-derived representations are inputs to higher-level functions like allocation of attention and integration with information from other modalities.

Learners who are blind or have a visual impairment will use touch for gaining information. They gain information through tactile materials, including diagrams, graphs, maps and real objects. A student who is totally blind will need to develop tactile skills and learn to read and write in Braille. All learners with visual impairment will need to develop listening skills for use so that they can concentrate on and interpret important sound information first.

English Braille is a complex code and there is more to learn than when using print, as seen in Chapter 5. Some children acquire Japanese Braille first, but all

English Braille users must learn the complex rules. The code does impose heavy cognitive load on the learner. Reading in Braille requires all the skills of reading, including blending, memory, using syntax, and sequencing. Reading Braille is essentially the process of reading, attaching meaning to symbols.

Another issue is the use of fingers and the way in which the brain can perceive the tactile shapes that represent letters. This involves training the fingers and hands to move efficiently over pages of Braille and teaching the brain to make sense of the raised dots that make up the Braille code. Even with excellent teaching and practice, Braille readers are likely to achieve a slower reading speed than print readers, typically 80 – 100 wpm as opposed to 200 – 250 wpm.

To help learners improve their speed of reading, two main types of activities are proposed. The first type focuses on the meaning of the text and encourages the use of syntactic and semantic information to anticipate the likely words, phrases or meaning in a passage. This approach is used with print reading, but it may well be more critical for a Braille reader who might be unable to read efficiently without this support. A second type of activity uses many speed reading techniques, such as skimming, scanning, key words, and section headings. With practice, an exercise in which a reader could try to follow several lines with several fingers simultaneously would enable the reader to make some sense of paragraphs without reading every word. This requires good finger control and the ability to read without feeling the need to examine every word. However, listening to accelerated recordings might be the fastest way to obtain information nowadays.

Chapter 8

Teachers' voices from blind schools in Japan

Introduction

Recently, it has been widely said that learning English is important for everybody given the demands for communication skills in a globalised modern society, including the internet. It is more important for visually impaired people to learn English in order to enhance their potential and reduce the gap caused by lack of sight. Visual impairment affects every aspect of human life and all domains of human activities. Mastering English becomes a sort of bridge through which visually impaired people can have access to different cultures and different opportunities in society.

Until the 1990's, Japan's foreign language education had focused on translation-orientated reading skills, but recently, the importance of the attainment of communication skills has been emphasised. Teachers realised that listening and speaking skills need to be taught thoroughly in the classroom. However, teaching the English Braille system at blind schools takes a very long time and requires a lot of effort, which leads to the lack of communicative activities at many schools.

In this chapter, I report on the raw data in my research for the Japanese government concerning the teaching of foreign languages, particularly English, in Japanese secondary schools for the blind, on the basis of questionnaires and interviews conducted in schools for the blind.

8.1. Background

Sixty blind schools all over Japan took part in this project. Forty-nine junior high school teachers who teach beginners and fifty-seven senior high school teachers who teach intermediate learners participated in the questionnaire in September 2013. Most teachers were not trained specifically for blind schools and had taught there less than five years.

English is taught for a maximum of four periods per week, in total 200 minutes, by using a censored textbook by the Ministry of Education. Although there are various censored textbooks available in print, there is only one in Braille. Teachers produce supplementary materials and tests in Braille by themselves. The National Institute of Special Needs Education (NISE) provides support and training for teachers.

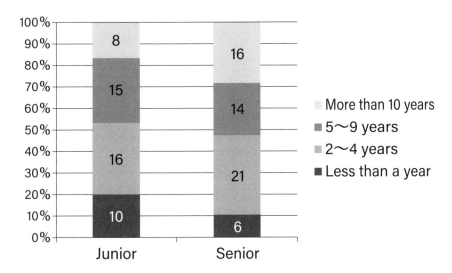

Figure 8-1. Number of years taught at blind schools

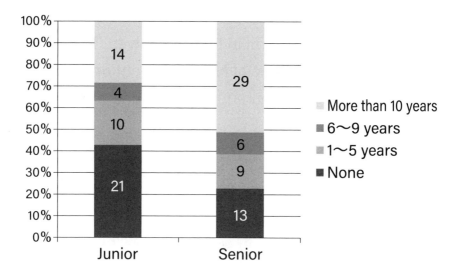

Figure 8-2. Number of years taught at other schools

8.2. Teaching reading skills by touch

It is widely recognised that sound/pronunciation patterns and spelling should be taught simultaneously to beginners. Although teachers who have more than five years of experience at blind schools adopt phonics and other letter-sound connection techniques, poorly experienced teachers pay little attention to sounds when teaching spelling in Braille.

Many teachers find it time-consuming to teach English spelling in Braille because of its complexity. As we saw in Sections 5.2.2 and 5.2.3, second grade Braille rules are extremely confusing, and Japanese ways of pronouncing Braille transfer to English, which causes serious learning problems for beginners. These students have to learn new spellings along with the meanings and different pronunciations at the same time.

While English native speakers have acquired the sound systems and meanings before starting to learn Braille, foreign language learners do not have phonological knowledge of their target language. Learning Braille, sounds and meanings at the same time poses a serious problem for beginners, and some students become demotivated as a result.

8.2.1. On the confusion of Japanese and English Braille systems

Overall, beginners tend to confuse Japanese and English Braille systems more than intermediate and advanced learners, but when English and Japanese Braille are used in instructions of textbooks or examinations, many elementary and some intermediate students become confused.

It seems that exposure to English Braille is crucial. In particular, teachers point out that punctuation is the most problematic. In addition, beginners tend to memorise spellings with Japanese sounds, for instance, 'play' as /ne-ni-a-mu/. Some intermediate students read out a sequence in a Japanese way, but it does not make sense at all, and so they re-read it in an English way, but unknown English words often hinder the reading process. Their reading speed is slow because of these reasons.

8.2.2. How to handle unknown words in a text

The most accepted popular strategy is to touch before and after the unknown word and guess its meaning (27 junior and 39 senior high school teachers). A similar strategy is to finish the sentence even if students are facing unknown words, and infer their meaning by spelling or by activating knowledge of phonics (14 junior and 18 senior high school teachers). Some teachers ask the students to notice the parts of speech (4 junior and 5 senior high school teachers), or to just ignore new words and proceed with reading (10 junior and 1 senior high school teachers).

Students who have difficulty in proceeding with reading will ask for help, and teachers show a phrase as one unit. Many teachers find it more effective to introduce new words first, and then read aloud the passage that contains them.

8.2.3. Sound-letter relationships and Braille

It has been emphasised that spelling instruction should raise and accompany phonological awareness. The following figures summarise how teachers connect spelling and sound in the classroom.

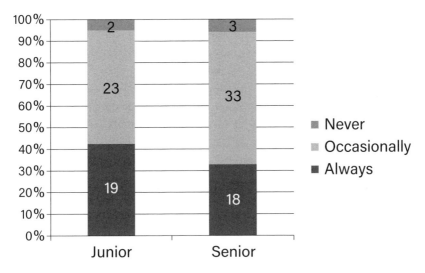

Figure 8-3. Explain rules for sounds and spelling by phonics

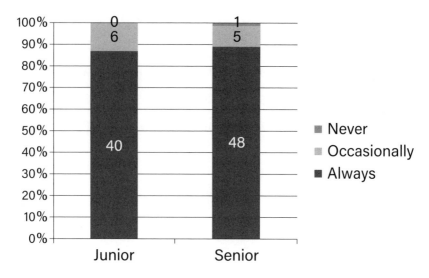

Figure 8-4. Touch Braille and pronounce

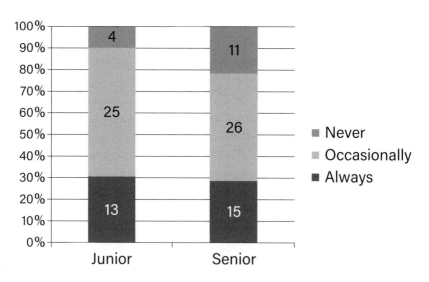

Figure 8-5. Spell by Braille and pronounce

Chapter 8 Teachers' voices from blind schools in Japan 289

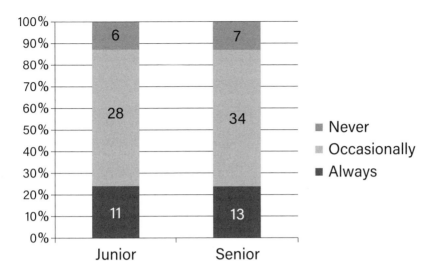

Figure 8-6. Spell by Braille after listening to sounds

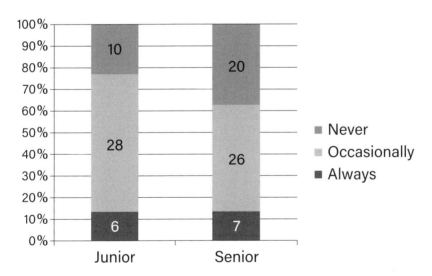

Figure 8-7. Spell by Braille via translation

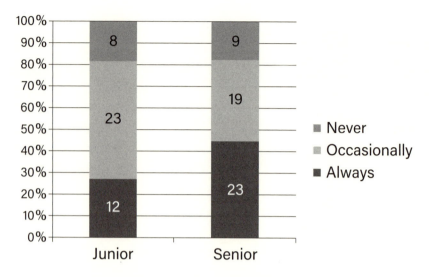

Figure 8-8. Read out Braille text

Other comments are as follows. Many students are encouraged to practise reading out the textbook at home. Some teachers minimize Braille use and teach English orally, as some students do not concentrate on Braille reading or prefer oral communication tasks.

8.2.4. How to check students' ability of Braille reading

The following two approaches are very common. Firstly, let them pronounce or read out Braille texts (40 junior and 45 senior high school teachers). Secondly, let them spell Braille with a brailler (35 junior and 35 senior high school teachers).

Some teachers produce a word list in Braille, and let their students check whether the words are spelt correctly, focusing on spelling in full and contractions. Others encourage the trial and error approach, letting students read the same text several times or copy and write the text by themselves. Most teachers pay great attention to the full spelling and contracted spelling at the same time. These activities are unnecessary for normal-sighted students, and teachers are struggling with the timing of instruction.

8.3. Teaching listening skills

For blind students, listening is the most essential and important skill for communication. It is natural for them to learn a foreign language through listening, but listening and speaking skills have not been taught sufficiently at schools, firstly because the purpose and the goal of foreign language teaching in Japan have been reading skills by means of translation, and secondly because recording technologies have been developing. The attainment of Braille reading skills has been the major aim of foreign language teaching at blind schools.

8.3.1. Use of audio programmes in the classroom

Conscientious teachers try hard to use sound materials in the classroom. They play supplementary audio CDs and read out the text by themselves. Those who answered 'never' mentioned that their schools do not have a CD player or audio programmes. In actuality, a CD player is affordable and many people have their own player, so these teachers seem to find no reason to teach listening.

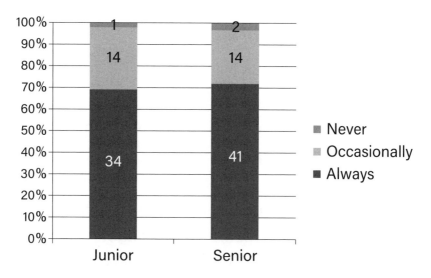

Figure 8-9. Frequency of the use of sound materials

8.3.2. Listening to passages or conversations with several paragraphs

In order to develop listening skills, students need to listen to longer passages or conversations. The following figure shows how they learn listening skills.

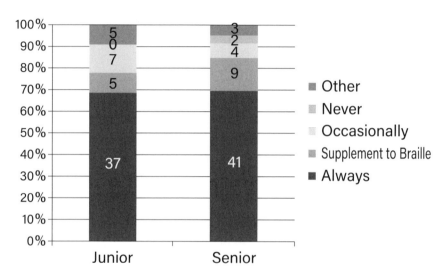

Figure 8-10. Listening training with longer texts

Many teachers use the censored textbook as a listening material: they play the attached CD and check comprehension. The disadvantage of this way of instruction is that some texts are too difficult for students to follow, because many texts consist of written forms with complicated sentence structures for reading rather than colloquial styles. Some teachers use other listening-focused materials.

Students like to talk with other students and with their teacher, and teachers use context- and situation-based communication activities with background sound effects. Assistant language teachers, native speakers of English, sometimes visit and speak to them, which is reported to be very effective and popular.

8.3.3. Braille and listening

Many teachers seek ways to integrate Braille reading and listening activities. There are some options. The most popular approach is to play the attached CD of the reading passages in the textbook (28 junior and 41 senior high school teachers). Some teachers use different materials for listening from reading, i.e. listening-focused supplementary coursebooks (9 junior and 9 senior high school teachers).

However, some teachers do not teach listening skills at all, focusing only on Braille reading (15 junior and 9 senior high school teachers).

Other options are as follows. Some teachers produce tape scripts in Braille and let students read after/while they listen ('touch & listen' or 'listen & touch' practice). Many teachers read out materials and encourage students to do so too.

There are contradictory opinions. Some teachers say that there is no time to spare for listening, while others insist that listening is more important than Braille reading. These teachers all agree that the lack of time for English language teaching is very serious, so they cannot teach the four language skills at blind schools. This is because the curriculum is not designed for the disabled.

8.3.4. Time for listening activities

Teachers wish to teach listening as well as reading, but since Braille reading takes time, they have little time left for listening activities. The following figure summarises the reality in the classroom.

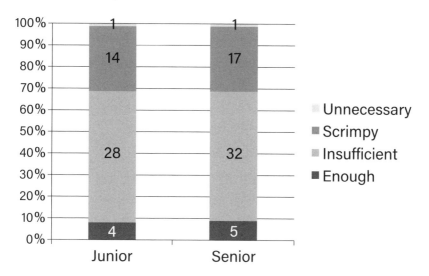

Figure 8-11. Instruction time for listening

8.3.5. Homework

Assignments are necessary for foreign language learning. The following homework is common.

- Workbook
  (28 junior and 33 senior high school teachers)
- Braille reading
  (25 junior and 22 senior high school teachers)
- Read aloud
  (23 junior and 28 senior high school teachers)
- Translation
  (16 junior and 16 senior high school teachers)

<Other activities>
- Copy/write passages in the textbook
- Check new words
- Memorise words, phrases, and sentences
- Grammar exercises
- Type sentences and use screen reader to practise listening and pronunciation
- Memorise words by using 'listen & repeat' word books
- Braille writing practice with brailler and/or computer
- Keeping a diary in English (recording and/or Braille)

8.3.6. Students' reactions to listening activities

Although students need to learn to read in Braille, they might feel confident in listening. Teachers' impressions are summarised in the following figure.

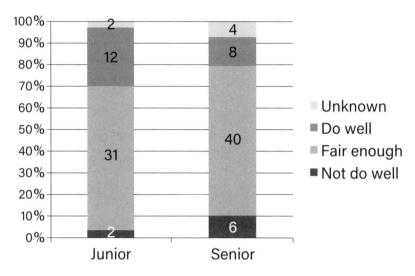

Figure 8-12. Listening ability of longer texts

Teachers' comments are as follows. Totally blind students are superior to weak-sighted students in listening. Blind students in particular are good at listening to conversations. There are individual differences, but sighted students are no better at listening than visually impaired students. Even if blind students cannot take notes as sighted students can, they seem to be able to understand long passages well in their phonological memory. Teachers sense that students are likely to develop high proficiency in listening and speaking skills if good instruction is provided.

8.4. Teaching speaking skills

At some blind schools, there are few numbers of students learning there, and it is sometimes very difficult to practise speaking skills among students. In this case, a student and a teacher talk in English. The vast majority of teachers encourage students to speak in English (47 junior and 55 senior high school teachers). When they teach pronunciation, they focus on how to make sounds (place and manner of articulation) by oral explanation and/or touch (44 junior and 49 senior high school teachers).

According to some teachers, students who listen to pronunciations of native speakers all the time tend to attain accurate and fluent skills. Moreover, if blind students are interested in pronunciation, they will be good speakers of English.

Many teachers notice that their students become fluent speakers of English soon (34 junior and 33 senior high school teachers). They believe that blind students have 'sensitive ears'. Students are able to repeat foreign sounds accurately, and they concentrate on sounds very carefully. Some teachers fear that the instructors' regional and foreign accents severely influence students' pronunciation. Teachers try hard to practise pronunciation and to develop listening skills by themselves to provide accurate instruction.

However, if students do not have sufficient opportunities to listen to and speak English at junior high school because of the Braille-oriented reading instruction, their oral fluency will be limited. In particular, 'touch & read out' activities are not suitable for fluency development because of the decoding time it requires. These students tend to pronounce with a Japanese accent and their listening ability lags behind.

8.4.1. Teachers' attitudes toward speaking skills

While many teachers think it is necessary to teach speaking skills, there are barriers in reality: limitation of time, students' motivation, preparation for entrance examinations, etc. If teachers believe that speaking is unnecessary, their students will have no opportunity to talk in English. This sometimes happens at blind schools, and students experience a loss. The following figure summarises teachers' opinions.

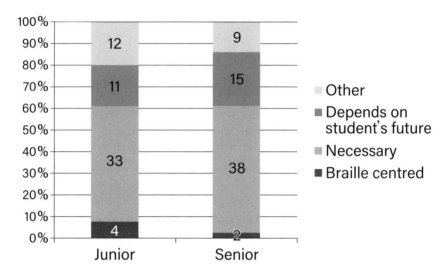

Figure 8-13. Necessity of listening and speaking skills

Other comments are as follows. Teachers have to teach Braille reading and listening/speaking skills, but they are struggling with time pressures and realistic issues, such as Braille-centred entrance examinations. Many teachers are aware that blind students like a communicative approach because of its necessity and naturalness. If teachers consider their futures as blind citizens, they find it important to teach communication skills in English, but they do not know how to close the gap.

8.4.2. Providing a proper balance of the four language skills

Ideally, everyone agrees that the four language skills need to be taught, but it is not easy to realise in a foreign language environment where English is not used daily.

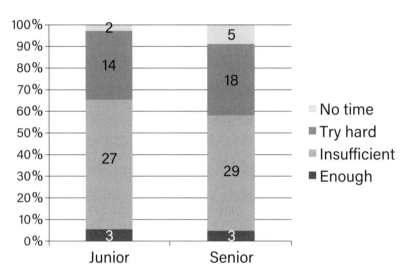

Figure 8-14. Time for the four language skills

For elementary and intermediate students, Braille reading puts an extra burden on learning, because they have to learn spelling in full and rules for contractions. This is why they need more time to be able to read English texts in Braille. If teachers tackle this issue in the classroom, they will have insufficient time.

To make matters worse, students get bored if they learn Braille all the time. They are more motivated about communication than Braille techniques. Some teachers focus more on listening and speaking than reading skills. Teachers wonder what the best method of instruction is for the happiness of their students, because they will need communication skills if they live overseas or select a job that requires English; however, ironically, these skills are excluded in order to prepare students for passing entrance examinations in Japan, in which Braille reading skills are crucial.

8.4.3. Necessity of providing speaking instruction

In Japan, many people think it unnecessary to learn listening and speaking skills of a foreign language because there is no opportunity to communicate with others in the language. They claim that reading skills by means of translation are the most necessary in this country. Some teachers support this 'anti communication' attitude, which influences their classroom.

However, the role of foreign language teaching is to gradually develop the four language skills of learners, whether it is communicative or not. Learners need a well balance of the four language skills if they wish to use the learned language as a 'language'. This is why the Ministry of Education has clearly stated since the 1960's that the four language skills must be taught at all levels, but people's faith in the translation method and the lack of techniques have blocked this. The following figure summarises teachers' attitudes today.

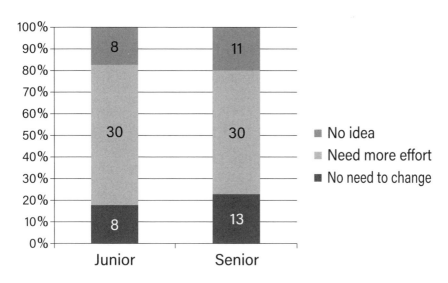

Figure 8-15. Possibility of providing listening and speaking instruction

Some teachers complain that the general intelligence of students is declining or that the family environment is unsatisfactory. In some rural areas, students have no chance to meet foreigners, and they are demotivated in foreign language learning.

In addition to these social problems, many teachers nowadays question the heavily Braille-oriented approach for every student. There are individual differences in the use of Braille, motivation, future vision, family expectations, etc. It is true that Japanese Braille is essential to educate students, but we should reconsider whether all the students need to learn English Braille completely. Since the shortage of time is very serious, teachers cannot shift their attention to a particular skill in the classroom.

8.4.4. Opportunities to interact with native speakers of English

Many teachers suppose that it is necessary for students to have opportunities to communicate with native speakers of English. Students are reported to really enjoy communicative tasks with them. Experiences in actual language use, face-to-face interactions, are driving forces of learning. However, the opportunities of learning with native speakers are varied from place to place. Some schools have ample chances while others do not.

Activities in the classroom include the following.

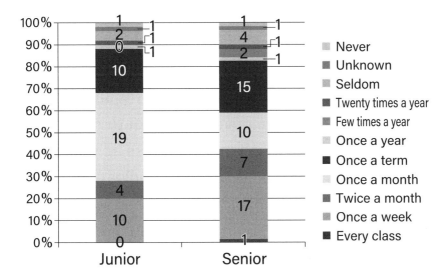

Figure 8-16. Frequency of visits by native speakers

- Team teaching
  (31 junior and 40 senior high school teachers)
- Games
  (31 junior and 40 senior high school teachers)
- Pronunciation exercises
  (25 junior and 24 senior high school teachers)

<Other activities>
- English conversation   • Short talks   • Role play
- Comprehension practice   • Dictation
- Giving a speech
- Self-introduction and other cultural topics

8.5. Issues in foreign language teaching at blind schools

The main purpose of Japan's English language teaching used to be the development of the learner's ability to translate English into Japanese accurately, but now it is to communicate with people in English properly. In order to achieve this goal, the four language skills need to be taught gradually in the curriculum.

    Teachers plan for the learning and development of all the learners they encounter in their school or setting. This is an ongoing and essential process illustrated as follows (Smidt, 2009: 8):

Table 8-1. Planning cycle for better learning and teaching

1. Gathering evidence about the learner.
2. Making sense of the evidence. What does it tell us?
3. Based on what has been learned, plan what to do next.
4. Putting the plan into practice.
5. Evaluating what happened.

8.5.1. On spelling and Braille

Traditionally, written texts have been widely used from the very beginning, which has caused serious learning problems for beginners. Learners in the process of cognitive development find it impossible to learn a new writing system, a new sound system, and new meanings together at the same time.

At blind schools, students must learn the English Braille system, which is completely different from the Japanese one. English and Japanese Braille assign different sounds, which is really troublesome. Teachers and students spend a long time mastering the new Braille system, including first and second grade rules. They are required to master spelling in full and contracted forms within a few years.

Although native speakers of English have acquired English through sounds, Japanese learners of English have to learn spellings, sounds and meanings at the same time. Literacy research has revealed that language acquisition proceeds from sounds to letters, but not vice versa. It is more natural and less effortful to learn language through sounds first, and then to symbolise the sounds by means of letters. Many researchers propose that phonological awareness play an important role in literacy, as discussed in Chapter 5.

At blind schools, Braille texts are introduced from the beginning, and students have no time to get used to the sound system of English before learning spelling. Students have been encouraged to 'touch & pronounce' English. At first, students tend to read out in Japanese ways, then as alphabet letter, and by phonetically correct ways. Native speakers of English who have acquired English sounds can guess word meanings from context, so contractions help them speed up reading, but foreign language learners face tough challenges.

Some learners and teachers give way to listening and speaking activities and give up Braille reading. In particular, late blind students who are learning Japanese Braille or have not mastered it and those who have other mental or physical disabilities find the Braille system a barrier.

In addition, many sighted teachers at blind schools have not mastered Braille at all. They are learning it with blind students by sight. Because teachers do not know Braille, they feel unconfident and uncomfortable in teaching English Braille reading. Most teachers are suddenly ordered to go to a blind school without specific training, and to go back to junior or senior high school after five years or so when they get to know English Braille and how to teach English to visually impaired students. Teaching methodologies, materials, and support are desperately required.

8.5.2. On listening and speaking skills

It has been commonly believed that reading and translation skills are the most important for Japanese learners of English. This is because the vast majority of Japanese people do not have chances to communicate in English in their daily lives. At blind schools, the main focus has been on reading in Braille in order to prepare for entrance examinations.

However, some blind students go abroad or work for companies or institutions where a high command of English is required. To broaden their future possibilities, communication skills in English need to be taught as well. Oral communication is crucial if a visually impaired person needs assistance in English speaking countries, but Braille skills will not help. They must express themselves in English and understand what the kind person assisting them is telling them.

In addition, technological development has enabled visually impaired people to communicate by means of sound recognition systems. Screen readers read out information on the monitor, and speech software creates texts when speaking into a microphone. Recent screen readers produce natural and fluent pronunciation. Blind students will have more opportunities to listen to English than to read in Braille.

In English speaking countries, various pieces of information are provided by audio devices, because many visually impaired people, including the late blind, find it much easier to access sounds than Braille. Thanks to the development of OCR (optical character recognition) technology, visually impaired students can read many academic books by ear without waiting for them to be made in Braille.

Medical and cognitive studies have shown that the four language skills are processed differently in our brain, and each skill develops on its own right. Receptive and productive vocabularies are acquired, stored and activated differently. However, some teachers believe that if they teach reading skills, students will be able to listen to, write, and speak English. This common view is scientifically unsupported. The four language skills need to be taught in the classroom. Braille reading is nothing but a receptive skill, and students should be provided with listening and speaking activities as well. Development of communication skills in English is required for visually impaired students to guarantee their future options. The development of ICT (Information and Communications Technology) enables students to communicate with others in a network, and some schools use CALL for interactive learning opportunities.

Some teachers insist that Braille reading and translation skills will suffice, but recent findings in brain sciences have revealed that reading is controlled and back-upped by auditory systems. The smooth flow of Braille encoding by touch is enhanced by sound processors in the brain. There are a few reasons why listening skills are necessary. It seems to me that this claim is accepted outside Japan, but people who have learned foreign languages by translation are not convinced and see no value or necessity of listening and speaking skills. My life as a blind person has shown me that translation skills in Braille are insufficient to broaden the future of visually impaired people, but communication skills in English will.

8.5.3. On teaching blind children English

Under the recent national curriculum in Japan, English has to be taught at all primary schools. Japanese teachers and parents like to teach children the letters and spellings from the very beginning. They do not care about sounds, pronouncing English with a strong Japanese accent. This approach is not recommended, firstly because many children find it complicated and puzzling to process letters, and secondly because phonetic and phonological awareness of English has not been acquired properly.

In the process of language acquisition, children acquire sound systems unconsciously, so the quality and quantity of input are critical. If teachers and parents provide accented speech frequently, children will imitate and acquire it, which is stored in their implicit knowledge and become resilient to unlearning.

At blind schools, since the lack of time for English language teaching is very serious, teachers feel satisfied in teaching English Braille to children. Unfortunately, this is really problematic, as children are in the process of acquiring Japanese Braille. Together with the mysterious sounds of English, children become confused and demotivated. At primary schools, listening and oral communication activities should be focused on rather than Braille reading.

One common misunderstanding in Japan is to rely heavily on phonics all the time from the very beginning. Phonics was originally recommended to English speaking children who have acquired sound systems of English. Phonics is helpful to understand how sounds are spelt under the rules.

Teachers must remember that this method was not developed for foreign language learners who have to handle new sounds, new letters, and new meanings at the same time (Kuhn & Levy, 2015). Children under cognitive development do not process these three elements at once. Many of them cannot catch up and lose interest. Languages are naturally acquired as sound systems. Reading and spelling instruction should be introduced afterwards.

Literate adults feel uneasy if they do not use letters around. It is true that adults who have completed cognitive development can process new sounds, letters and meanings at the same time, but they need to know that the cognition of children is totally different from theirs. Especially at blind schools, children require rich English input in good quality, such as with General American or Received Pronunciation. Strong accents should be avoided when learners are creating a foreign language processor in their phonological loop of working memory.

Regarding pronunciation, many sighted teachers explain articulation in words, but blind learners do not fully understand what they are learning. There are limitations to oral explanations, because learners do not see precisely how to control their articulators. Sighted people create spatial representations by vision, and blind people do by touch, as we saw in Chapter 4.

Some teachers succeed by using a prop, such as an alligator that has a big mouth with teeth and a tongue or a plastic model of a jaw with teeth and a tongue, which is commonly used for teeth brushing exercises. In Japan, nurses occasionally show pupils how to brush their teeth by using a big jaw model and a large toothbrush. If blind children touch the lips, teeth, and tongue to notice how to pronounce sounds, such as 'f' or 'th', they can master English sounds with ease.

Many teachers are aware that while sighted students confuse 's' and 'th', blind learners pronounce 'th' as 'f' like native speakers of English. Blind students sense friction by ear even though they cannot see teeth and tongue movements. By touching articulators, they create spatial representations accurately. Just as sighted learners benefit from diagrams or pictures to check places and manners of articulation, 3D figures or plastic models are necessary for blind learners.

Teachers and parents are often surprised at visually impaired children's accurate and quick reactions to sounds. They can accurately mimic sounds immediately. My experiences tell me that blind people, including myself, react to all high and low frequency sounds constantly in auditory acuity tests. Doctors and nurses often suspect that we watch when they turn on the device. Of course, blind people do not see what they are doing.

According to past studies, the acuity level seems to be the same among sighted and blind populations. Even if the final results are similar among them, I propose that the reaction time data would tell us something as well. Blind people attend and react to sounds accurately as soon as they perceive them. Similarly, normal-sighted people can identify shapes immediately when they see them in vision tests (a chromatic acuity chart), but visually impaired people need some time to respond. Although the percentage of correctness might be the same, the time lag will mean something in our daily lives. This is why I suppose that reaction time is important in visual and auditory research.

Reaction time measures have been popular procedures in psychology and other fields since the 1980's and have been used to address a range of issues that include retrieval of information from memory, parallel and serial information processing, the psychological representation of semantic and logical representations, naming and letter classification tasks, and selective attention. The measures themselves are topics of research as well, seeking to understand what factors could cause or account for variation in reaction times, especially with respect to speed-accuracy trade-off and implicit learning (Leow, 2015: Chapter 8).

8.5.4. Teacher's roles

Moreno (2010: 5) suggests four elements that make up the complexity of the teaching profession.

1. **Teaching is never routine.**
   Teachers must constantly deal with changing students and curriculum, learning needs, questions and dilemmas, while they might feel that their yearly cycle is a regular routine.
2. **Teaching has multiple goals.**
   Teachers need to address at the same time students' intellectual, social and emotional development.

3. **Teaching is done in relationship with a diversity of learners.**
   Teachers need to orchestrate the needs of a group of students who are diverse in terms of their strengths, backgrounds, areas for improvement and special needs.
4. **Teaching requires the integration of several knowledge types.**
   Teachers need to continually combine their knowledge about development, subject matter, individual and group pedagogies, and learner diversity to promote the learning of all students.

According to pedagogical research, teachers draw from different sources of professional knowledge and specific skills make for effective teachers.

Table 8-2. Types of knowledge and skills to be an effective teacher

Professional knowledge	Professional skills
Content knowledge	Planning skills
Pedagogical knowledge	Communication skills
Knowledge about learners	Motivation skills
	Classroom management skills
Knowledge about curriculum	Assessment skills
	Technology skills

8.5.5. Final comments

This chapter looked at issues in English language teaching at blind schools based on questionnaires and interviews. This last section summarises the implications for education.

Firstly, teaching materials in Braille and supplementary teaching aids are urgently required. This has been a long-lasting problem. Teachers all over Japan produce materials by themselves, but when they leave blind schools nothing is shared, because no institution is in charge of English language teaching for visually impaired students. Some teachers even consider their materials as precious possessions. Teachers' experiences should be recorded, analysed and widely disseminated.

Secondly, professional training and support are required. Most teachers know nothing about blindness and Braille when they are ordered to go to a blind school. Surprisingly, some teachers feel that they have been sent to a blind school as punishment by the authorities. Practical training as well as education on the theoretical background of psychological and cognitive aspects of visual impairment should be provided before they start teaching. At present, teachers 'live and learn' at blind schools. In addition, phonetics and phonology of English must be studied carefully in order to provide good input to blind learners who tend to absorb sounds sensitively.

In addition, recent national surveys suggest that people with visual impairment can be broadly divided into two distinct groups: a group of learners with visual impairment and no additional difficulties, and a larger group who have visual impairment in combination with a range of additional difficulties. While the overall population of people with visual impairment appears to be more or less constant, the proportion of learners with additional disabilities within this population is forecast to increase. This increase can be partly linked to recent improvements in medical knowledge and techniques, which have resulted in a changing pattern in the medical conditions of learners. Learners with visual impairment in combination with additional disabilities present a special challenge to professionals responsible for their education. Teachers in a mainstream classroom will need to have knowledge of the particular educational needs created by the unique combination of the difficulties as well as an understanding of how best these needs can be addressed within an appropriate learning environment (Arter, et al., 1999: Chapter 6).

Thirdly, explicit knowledge about speech and language is not sufficient for fluent communication. Teaching and learning how to pronounce by means of oral or tactile approaches do not necessarily guarantee fluency. Students need to practise and attain sensorimotor skills. Correct use of articles, numbers, and other grammar rules must be accessed rapidly to maintain accurate and fluent communication. Since opportunities for English communication are extremely limited in a foreign language environment, exposure to English and frequent oral practice are crucial in Japan. ICT is probably the best way for achieving these goals.

Lastly, opportunities of communicating with native speakers of English should be guaranteed. All learners of English, whether they are blind or not and whether they live in big cities or rural areas, have the equal right to receive the best possible education. It is effective for visually impaired students to learn by means of auditory input in communicative environments. Many teachers have reported that blind students are really looking forward to talking with native speakers, while fewer students with normal eyesight enjoy oral communication tasks.

Concluding Remarks

The purpose of this book was to review what has been proposed in the field of cognitive science, including linguistics, phonetics and phonology, on the acquisition and learning of languages, with special reference to visually impaired people. It is clear that people can acquire languages without vision by means of auditory and haptic sensations. What is the role of vision in language learning?

Vision sometimes enhances and hinders language learning and processing. Normal-sighted people can see the speaker's mouth moving, which helps them interpret the sounds accurately, but there are some occasions when visual stimuli may cause illusions that lead to misunderstandings.

Blind people are able to attain native-like pronunciations in a foreign language, which means that the auditory system is reliable enough to control articulation without vision. Explicit knowledge of place and manner of articulation may be of help in articulation, but we cannot explain how we instantly perceive sounds and decode meanings from the sound sequences. It might be useful to know how to produce sounds of a foreign language, but it is too simplistic to claim that such explicit knowledge guarantees accurate and fluent production.

It has been reported that infants watch their parents' mouth movements to acquire articulation. What they are doing is building up mechanisms to control articulators by only looking. However, we know that blind infants can acquire the same system without vision. Rich auditory input controls articulation automatically and unconsciously. In the process of first language acquisition, the environment provides necessary and sufficient input, whilst in foreign language learning environments, the quality and quantity of input must be considered seriously. This is where the significance of explicit learning comes in.

By researching individuals who lack a particular sensory modality, we can understand much more clearly how each sense contributes to learning. As a result, precise scientific implications can be provided for teaching and learning. I would like to find ways to put theoretical findings into practice in the field of education and social welfare.

References

A

Afflerbach, P. (ed.) (2016) *Handbook of Individual Differences in Reading*. New York: Routledge

Aitkin, S., Buultjens, M., Clark, C., Eyre, J. and Pease, L. (2000) *Teaching Children who are Deafblind*. London: David Fulton

Albertazzi, L., van Tonder, G. and Vishwanath, D. (eds.) (2010) *Perception beyond Inference: The Information Content of Visual Processes*. Cambridge: MIT Press

ARAL (Annual Review of Applied Linguistics) Volume 32 (2012) Special issue on formulaic language

Arbib, M. (ed.) (2013) *Language, Music, and the Brain*. Cambridge: Cambridge University Press

Archibald, J. (1998) *Second Language Phonology*. Amsterdam: John Benjamins

Arter, C., Mason, H., McCall, S., McLinden, M. and Stone, J. (1999) *Children with Visual Impairment in Mainstream*

Settings. London: David Fulton

Ashby, M. and Maidment, J. (2005) *Introducing Phonetic Science*. Cambridge: Cambridge University Press

Astesano, C. and Jucla, M. (eds.) (2015) *Neuropsycholinguistic Perspectives on Language Cognition*. Hove: Psychology Press

B

Baars, B. and Gage, N. (2013) *Fundamentals of Cognitive Neuroscience*. Waltham: Elsevier

Bacci, F. and Melcher, D. (eds.) (2013) *Art and the Senses*. Oxford: Oxford University Press

Bailly, G., Perrier, P. and Vatikiotis-Bateson, E. (eds.) (2012) *Audiovisual Speech Processing*. Cambridge: Cambridge University Press

Ball, M. and Duckworth, M. (eds.) (1996) *Advances in Clinical Phonetics*. Amsterdam: John Benjamins

Ball, M. and Gibbon, F. (eds.) (2013) *Handbook of Vowels and Vowel Disorders*. New York: Psychology Press

Ball, M. and Müller, N. (2005) *Phonetics for Communication Disorders*. Mahwah: Lawrence Erlbaum

Ball, M., Müller, N. and Rutter, B. (2010) *Phonology for Communication Disorders*. New York: Psychology Press

Ball, M., Perkins, M., Müller, N. and Howard, S. (eds.) (2008) *The Handbook of Clinical Linguistics*. Oxford: Blackwell

Ballesteros, S. and Heller, M. (eds.) (2004) *Touch, Blindness and Neuroscience*. Universidad Nacional De Educacion A Dostancia

Bannan, N. (ed.) (2012) *Music, Language, and Human Evolution*. Oxford: Oxford University Press

Barclay, L. (2012) *Learning to Listen/Listening to Learn: Teaching Listening Skills to Students with Visual Impairments*. New York: AFB Press

Bauman-Waengler, J. (2012) *Articulatory and Phonological Impairments* (4th edition). Boston: Pearson

Bermudez, J. (2014) *Cognitive Science* (2nd edition). Cambridge: Cambridge University Press

Best, A. (1992) *Teaching Children with Visual Impairments*. Milton Keynes: Open University Press

Birsh, J. (ed.) (2011) *Multisensory Teaching of Basic Language Skills* (3rd edition). Baltimore: Paul H. Brookes

Bishop, D. and Leonard, L. (eds.) (2000) *Speech and Language Impairment in Children: Causes, Characteristics, Intervention and Outcome*. New York: Psychology Press

Black, M. and Chiat, S. (2003) *Linguistics for Clinicians*. London: Arnold

Bohn, O. and Munro, M. (eds.) (2007) *Language Experience in Second Language Speech Learning: In Honor of James Emil Flege*. Amsterdam: John Benjamins

Bolhuis, J. and Everaert, M. (eds.) (2013) *Birdsong, Speech, and Language: Exploring the Evolution of Mind and Brain*. Cambridge: MIT Press

Bozic, N. and Murdoch, H. (eds.) (1996) *Learning through Interaction: Technology and Children with Multiple Disabilities*. London: David Fulton

Bremner, A., Lewkowicz, D. and Spence, C. (eds.) (2012) *Multisensory Development*. Oxford: Oxford University Press

Byrd, D. and Mintz, T. (2010) *Discovering Speech, Words, and Mind*. West Sussex: Wiley-Blackwell

C

Calvert, G., Spence, C. and Stein, B. (eds.) (2004) *The Handbook of Multisensory Processes*. Cambridge: MIT Press

Carey, S. (2009) *The Origin of Concepts*. Oxford: Oxford University Press

Cartwright, K. (2015) *Executive Skills and Reading Comprehension*. New York: Guilford Press

Cattaneo, Z. and Vecchi, T. (2011) *Blind Vision: The Neuroscience of Visual Impairment*. Cambridge: MIT Press

Chilton, P. (2014) *Language, Space and Mind: The Conceptual Geometry of Linguistic Meaning*. Cambridge: Cambridge

University Press

Chun, D. (2002) *Discourse Intonation in L2: From Theory and Research to Practice*. Amsterdam: John Benjamins

Collins, B. and Mees, I. (2013) *Practical Phonetics and Phonology (3rd edition)*. London: Routledge

Creagehead, N., Newman, P. and Secord, W. (1989) *Assessment and Remediation of Articulatory and Phonological Disorders (2nd edition)*. Columbus: Merrill Publishing Company

Cruttenden, A. (2008) *Gimson's Pronunciation of English (7th edition)*. London: Arnold

Crystal, D. (1981) *Clinical Linguistics*. Baltimore: Edward Arnold

Cummings, L. (2014) *The Communication Disorders Workbook*. Cambridge: Cambridge University Press

Cummings, L. (ed.) (2014) *The Cambridge Handbook of Communication Disorders*. Cambridge: Cambridge University Press

Curtis, W. (1987) *Clinical Management of Articulatory and Phonologic Disorders (2nd edition)*. Baltimore: Williams & Wilkins

Cutler, A. (2012) *Native Listening: Language Experience and the Recognition of Spoken Words*. Cambridge: MIT Press

D

Damico, J., Müller, N. and Ball, M. (eds.) (2010) *The Handbook of Language and Speech Disorders*. West Sussex: Wiley-Blackwell

Davis, B. (2015) *Spatial Reasoning in the Early Years*. New York: Routledge

Davis, B. and Zajdo, K. (eds.) (2008) *The Syllable in Speech Production*. New York: Lawrence Erlbaum

Daw, N. (2012) *How Vision Works: The Physiological Mechanisms behind What We See*. Oxford: Oxford University Press

Derwing, T. and Munro, M. (2015) *Pronunciation Fundamentals: Evidence-based Perspectives for L2 Teaching and Research*. Amsterdam: John Benjamins

Detheridge, T. and Detheridge, M. (2013) *Literacy through Symbols (2nd edition)*. London: Routledge

Deutsch, D. (ed.) (2013) *The Psychology of Music (3rd edition)*. Amsterdam: Elsevier

Divjak, D. and Gries, S. (eds.) (2012) *Frequency Effects in Language Representation*. Berlin: Mouton de Gruyter

Dodd, B. and Conn, L. (2000) 'The effect of Braille orthography on blind children's phonological awareness' *Journal of Research in Reading* 23: 1-11

Dunlea, A. (1989) *Vision and the Emergence of Meaning: Blind and Sighted Children's Early Language*. Cambridge:

Cambridge University Press

Durand, J. and Laks, B. (eds.) (2002) *Phonetics, Phonology, and Cognition*. Oxford: Oxford University Press

E

Eggermont, J. (2015) *Auditory Temporal Processing and its Disorders*. Oxford: Oxford University Press

Eilan, N., McCarthy, R. and Brewer, B. (eds.) (1993) *Spatial Representation: Problems in Philosophy and Psychology*. Oxford: Blackwell

Everest, A. and Pohlmann, K. (2009) *Master Handbook of Acoustics (5th edition)*. New York: McGraw Hill

Eysenck, M. and Keane, M. (2010) *Cognitive Psychology (6th edition)*. Hove: Psychology Press

F

Farris-Trimble, A. and Barlow, J. (eds.) (2014) *Perspectives on Phonological Theory and Development*. Amsterdam: John Benjamins

Fava, E. (ed.) (2002) *Clinical Linguistics: Theory and Applications in Speech Pathology and Therapy*. Amsterdam: John Benjamins

Ferrand, C. (2007) *Speech Science: An Integrated Approach to Theory and Clinical Practice (2nd edition)*. Boston: Pearson

Frisby, J. and Stone, J. (2010) *Seeing: The Computational Approach to Biological Vision (2nd edition)*. Cambridge: MIT Press

G

Gardenfors, P. (2014) *Geometry of Meaning: Semantics Based on Conceptual Spaces*. Cambridge: MIT Press

Gauker, C. (2011) *Words and Images: An Essay on the Origin of Ideas*. Oxford: Oxford University Press

Gick, B., Wilson, I. and Derrick, D. (2013) *Articulatory Phonetics*. Oxford: Blackwell

Gillon, G. (2004) *Phonological Awareness: From Research to Practice*. New York: Guilford Press

Gillon, G. and Young, A. (2002) 'The phonological-awareness skills of children who are blind' *Journal of Visual Impairment & Blindness* 96: 38-49

Godwin, D. and Perkins, M. (2002) *Teaching Language and Literacy in the Early Years (2nd edition)*. London: David Fulton

Goldrick, M., Ferreira, V. and Miozzo, M. (eds.) (2014) *The Oxford Handbook of Language Production*. Oxford: Oxford University Press

Goldstein, E. (ed.) (2005) *Blackwell Handbook of Sensation and Perception*. Oxford: Blackwell

Golper, L. (2010) *Medical Speech-Language Pathology (3rd*

edition). Delmar: Cengage

Goodale, M. and Milner, D. (2013) *Sight Unseen: An Exploration of Conscious and Unconscious Vision*. Oxford: Oxford University Press

Goodman, J. and Nusbaum, H. (eds.) (1994) *The Development of Speech Perception: The Transition from Speech Sounds to Spoken Words*. Cambridge: MIT Press

Green, A., Chapman, C., Kalaska, J. and Lepore, R. (eds.) (2011) *Enhancing Performance for Action and Perception: Multisensory Integration, Neuroplasticity and Neuroprosthetics*. Amsterdam: Elsevier

Gries, S. and Divjak, D. (eds.) (2012) *Frequency Effects in Language Learning and Processing*. Berlin: Mouton de Gruyter

Gulzow, I. and Gagarina, N. (eds.) (2007) *Frequency Effects in Language Acquisition: Defining the Limits of Frequency as an Explanatory Concept*. Berlin: Mouton de Gruyter

H

Hallam, S., Cross, I. and Thaut, M. (eds.) (2009) *The Oxford Handbook of Music Psychology*. Oxford: Oxford University Press

Hambrecht, G. and Rice, T. (2011) *Clinical Observation*. London: Jones & Bartlett

Handel, S. (1989) *Listening: An Introduction to the Perception* of Auditory Events. Cambridge: MIT Press

Hannahs, S. and Young-Scholten, M. (eds.) (1997) *Focus on Phonological Acquisition*. Amsterdam: John Benjamins

Hansen Edwards, J. and Zampini, M. (eds.) (2008) *Phonology and Second Language Acquisition*. Amsterdam: John Benjamins

Hardcastle, W., Laver, J. and Gibbon, F. (eds.) (2010) *The Handbook of Phonetic Sciences (2nd edition)*. Oxford: Wiley-Blackwell

Hargreaves, D. (1986) *The Developmental Psychology of Music*. Cambridge: Cambridge University Press

Harley, R., Truan, M. and Sanford, L. (1997) *Communication Skills for Visually Impaired Learners*. Springfield: Charles C. Thomas Publisher

Hartsuiker, R., Bastiaanse, R., Postma, A. and Wijnen, F. (eds.) (2005) *Phonological Encoding and Monitoring in Normal and Pathological Speech*. New York: Psychology Press

Hasegawa, Y. (2015) *Japanese: A Linguistic Introduction*. Cambridge: Cambridge University Press

Hatfield, G. and Allred, S. (eds.) (2012) *Visual Experience: Sensation, Cognition, and Constancy*. Oxford: Oxford University Press

Hatwell, Y., Streri, A. and Gentaz, E. (eds.) (2003) *Touching for Knowing: Cognitive Psychology of Haptic Manual Perception*. Amsterdam: John Benjamins

Hayes, L. and Flanigan, K. (2014) *Developing Word Recognition*. New York: Guilford Press

Heller, M. (ed.) (2000) *Touch, Representation, and Blindness*. Oxford: Oxford University Press

Heller, M. and Ballesteros, S. (eds.) (2006) *Touch and Blindness: Psychology and Neuroscience*. Mahwah: Lawrence Erlbaum

Heller, M. and Gentaz, E. (2014) *Psychology of Touch and Blindness*. Hove: Psychology Press

Hewings, M. (2004) *Pronunciation Practice Activities: A Resource Book for Teaching English Pronunciation*. Cambridge: Cambridge University Press

Hewlett, N. and Beck, J. (2006) *An Introduction to the Science of Phonetics*. Mahwah: Lawrence Erlbaum

Higgins, K. (2012) *The Music between Us: Is Music Universal Language?* Chicago: The University of Chicago Press

Hillis, A. (ed.) (2015) *The Handbook of Adult Language Disorders (2nd edition)*. New York: Psychology Press

Hodges, D. (ed.) (1996) *Handbook of Music Psychology (2nd edition)*. San Antonio: IMR Press

Hoffman, R., Hancock, P., Scerbo, M., Parasuraman, R. and Szalma, J. (eds.) (2015) *The Cambridge Handbook of Applied Perception Research*. Cambridge: Cambridge University Press

Horobin, S. (2013) *Does Spelling Matter?* Oxford: Oxford

University Press

Hulstijn, J. (2015) *Language Proficiency in Native and Non-native Speakers*. Amsterdam: John Benjamins

Hyvärinen, L. and Jacob, N. (2011) *What and How Does This Child See? Assessment of Visual Functioning for Development and Learning*. VISTEST Ltd

I

Ioup, G. and Weinberger, S. (eds.) (1987) *Interlangauge Phonology: The Acquisition of a Second Language Sound System*. Cambridge: Newbury House

J

Jackendoff, R. (2012) *A User's Guide to Thought and Meaning*. Oxford: Oxford University Press

James, A. (1988) *The Acquisition of a Second Language Phonology: A Linguistic Theory of Developing Sound Structures*. Tübingen: Gunter Narr Verlag

James, A. and Leather, J. (eds.) (1987) *Sound Patterns in Second Language Acquisition*. Dordrecht: Foris Publications

James, A. and Leather, J. (eds.) (1997) *Second-Language Speech: Structure and Process*. Berlin: Mouton de Gruyter

Johnson, A. and Jacobson, B. (2007) *Medical Speech-*

Language Pathology. New York: Thieme

Johnson, K. (2011) *Acoustic and Auditory Phonetics (3rd edition)*. Oxford: Blackwell

Johnson, K. and Schiffrar, M. (eds.) (2013) *People Watching: Social, Perceptual, and Neurophysiological Studies of Body Perception*. Oxford: Oxford University Press

Juffs, A. and Rodriguez, G. (2015) *Second Language Sentence Processing*. New York: Routledge

K

Keller, E. and Gopnik, M. (eds.) (1987) *Motor and Sensory Processes of Language*. Hillsdale: Lawrence Erlbaum

Kemmerer, D. (2015) *Cognitive Neuroscience of Language*. Hove: Psychology Press

Kent, R. (ed.) (1992) *Intelligibility in Speech Disorders*. Amsterdam: John Benjamins

Kent, R. and Read, C. (1992) *The Acoustic Analysis of Speech*. San Diego: Singular Publishing

Kiritani, S., Hirose, H. and Fujisaki, H. (eds.) (1997) *Speech Production and Language*. Berlin: Mouton de Gruyter

Kivy, P. (2007) *Music, Language, and Cognition*. Oxford: Clarendon Press

Knauff, M. (2013) *Space to Reason: A Spatial Theory of Human Thought*. Cambridge: MIT Press

Koelsch, S. (2012) *Brain and Music*. Oxford: Wiley-Blackwell

Kreiman, J. and Sidtis, D. (2011) *Foundations of Voice Studies: An Interdisciplinary Approach to Voice Production and Perception*. West Sussex: Wiley-Blackwell

Kuhn, M. and Levy, L. (2015) *Developing Fluent Reading: Teaching Fluency as a Foundational Skill*. New York: Guilford Press

Kusajima, T. (1983) *Braille Reading and Letter Reading*. Tokyo: Shu-ei-syuppan

L

Lacey, S. and Lawson, R. (eds.) (2013) *Multisensory Imagery*. New York: Springer

Ladefoged, P. (2012) *Vowels and Consonants (3rd edition)*. Oxford: Wiley-Blackwell

Ladefoged, P. and Johnson, K. (2015) *A Course in Phonetics (7th edition)*. Stamford: Cengage Learning

Lancaster, G. (2008) *Developing Speech and Language Skills*. London: Routledge

Landau, B. (ed.) (2013) *Understanding Cognitive Development: Approaches from Mind and Brain*. Oxon: Psychology Press

Landau, B. and Gleitman, L. (1985) *Language and Experience: Evidence from the Blind Child*. Cambridge: Harvard University Press

Landau, B. and Hoffman, J. (2012) *Spatial Representation:*

From Gene to Mind. Oxford: Oxford University Press

Lauwereyns, J. (2012) *Brain and the Gaze: On the Active Boundaries of Vision.* Cambridge: MIT Press

Leather, J. (ed.) (1999) *Phonological Issues in Language Learning.* London: Blackwell

Leow, R. (2015) *Explicit Learning in the L2 Classroom.* New York: Routledge

Lerdahl, F. and Jackendoff, R. (1983) *A Generative Theory of Tonal Music.* Cambridge: MIT Press

Lewis, M. and Wray, D. (2000) *Literacy in the Secondary School.* London: David Fulton

Lewis, V. and Collis, G. (eds.) (1997) *Blindness and Psychological Development in Young Children.* Leicester: BPS Books

Liberman, A. (1996) *Speech: A Special Code.* Cambridge: MIT Press

Lobner, S. (2013) *Understanding Semantics (2nd edition).* London: Routledge

Lum, C. (2002) *Scientific Thinking in Speech and Language Therapy.* New York: Psychology Press

M

Maassen, B. (ed.) (2010) *Speech Motor Control: New Developments in Basic and Applied Research.* Oxford: Oxford University Press

Major, M. (ed.) (1998) 'Interlanguage phonetics and phonology' Special issue *Studies in Second Language Acquisition 20*

Major, R. (2001) *Foreign Accent: The Ontogeny and Phylogeny of Second Language Phonology*. Mahwah: Lawrence Erlbaum

Maltby, M. and Knight, P. (2000) *Audiology*. London: David Fulton

Mareschal, D., Quinn, P. and Lea, S. (eds.) (2010) *The Making of Human Concepts*. Oxford: Oxford University Press

Margolis, E. and Laurence, S. (eds.) (1999) *Concepts: Core Readings*. Cambridge: MIT Press

Marr, D. (2010) *Vision: A Computational Investigation into the Human Representation and Processing of Visual Information*. Cambridge: MIT Press

Marschark, M., Tang, G. and Knoors, H. (eds.) (2015) *Bilingualism and Bilingual Deaf Education*. Oxford: Oxford University Press

Mason, H. and McCall, S. (eds.) (1997) *Visual Impairment: Access to Education for Children and Young People*. London: David Fulton

Mayer, C. and Trezek, B. (2015) *Early Literacy Development in Deaf Children*. Oxford: Oxford University Press

McLinden, M. and McCall, S. (2002) *Learning through Touch: Supporting Children with Visual Impairment and*

Additional Difficulties. London: David Fulton

Millar, S. (1994) *Understanding and Representing Space: Theory and Evidence from Studies with Blind and Sighted Children*. Oxford: Clarendon Press

Millar, S. (1997) *Reading by Touch*. London: Routledge

Millar, S. (2008) *Space and Sense*. Hove: Psychology Press

Mills, A. (1983) *Language Acquisition in the Blind Child: Normal and Deficient*. San Diego: College-Hill Press

Mithen, S. (2006) *The Singing Neanderthals: The Origin of Music, Language, Mind and Body*. Cambridge: Harvard University Press

Moore, B. (2013) *Introduction to the Psychology of Hearing (6th edition)*. Leiden: Brill

Moore, B., Tyler, L., and Marslen-Wilson, W. (eds.) (2009) *The Perception of Speech: From Sound to Meaning*. Oxford: Oxford University Press

Moreno, R. (2010) *Educational Psychology*. Hoboken: John Wiley & Sons

Moss, H. and Hampton, J. (eds.) (2003) *Conceptual Representation*. Hove: Psychology Press

Mourao, S. and Lourenco, M. (eds.) (2015) *Early Years Second Language Education*. London: Routledge

Moyer, A. (2013) *Foreign Accent: The Phenomenon of Non-native Speech*. New York: Cambridge University Press

Müller, N. and Ball, M. (eds.) (2013) *Research Methods in Clinical Linguistics and Phonetics*. Oxford: Blackwell

Murphy, G. (2002) *The Big Book of Concepts*. Cambridge: MIT Press

N

Nakamori, T. (2009) *Chunking and Instruction: The Place of Sounds, Lexis, and Grammar in English Language Teaching*. Tokyo: Hituzi Syobo

Newcombe, M. and Huttenlocher, J. (2000) *Making Space: The Development of Spatial Representation and Reasoning*. Cambridge: MIT Press

Nudds, M. and O'Callaghan, C. (eds.) (2009) *Sounds and Perception: New Philosophical Essays*. Oxford: Oxford University Press

Nussbaum, C. (2007) *The Musical Representation: Meaning, Ontology, and Emotion*. Cambridge: MIT Press

O

O'Kane, J. and Goldbart, J. (1998) *Communication before Speech*. London: David Fulton

Otake, T. and Cutler, A. (eds.) (1996) *Phonological Structure and Language Processing: Cross-Linguistic Studies*. Berlin: Mouton de Gruyter

P

Pagliano, P. (1999) *Multisensory Environments*. London: David Fulton

Pagliano, P. (2001) *Using a Multisensory Environment*. London: David Fulton

Pagliano, P. (2012) *The Multisensory Handbook*. London: Routledge

Parris, S. and Headley, K. (eds.) (2015) *Comprehension Instruction (3rd edition)*. New York: Guilford Press

Patel, A. (2008) *Music, Language, and the Brain*. Oxford: Oxford University Press

Pavlenko, A. (2014) *The Bilingual Mind: And What It Tells Us about Language and Thought*. Cambridge: Cambridge University Press

Peng, L. (2013) *Analyzing Sound Patterns: An Introduction to Phonology*. Cambridge: Cambridge University Press

Perez-Pereira, M. and Conti-Ramsden, G. (1999) *Language Development and Social Interaction in Blind Children*. Hove: Psychology Press

Pisoni, D. and Remez, R. (eds.) (2005) *The Handbook of Speech Perception*. Oxford: Blackwell

Plack, C. (ed.) (2010) *The Oxford Handbook of Auditory Science: Hearing*. Oxford: Oxford University Press

Plack, C. (2014) *The Sense of Hearing (2nd edition)*. New York: Psychology Press

Plomp, R. (2002) *The Intelligent Ear: On the Nature of Sound Perception*. New York: Psychology Press

Pollatsek, A. and Treiman, R. (eds.) (2015) *The Oxford Handbook of Reading*. Oxford: Oxford University Press

Popescu, I. (2009) *Word Frequency Studies*. Berlin: Mouton de Gruyter

Purves, D. and Lotto, B. (2011) *Why We See What We Do Redux: A Wholly Empirical Theory of Vision*. Sunderland: Sinauer Associates

Pylyshyn, Z. (2007) *Things and Places: How the Mind Connects with the World*. Cambridge: MIT Press

R

Rakison, D. and Oakes, L. (eds.) (2003) *Early Category and Concept Development*. Oxford: Oxford University Press

Rebuschat, P., Rohrmeier, M., Hawkins, J. and Cross, I. (eds.) (2012) *Language and Music as Cognitive Systems*. Oxford: Oxford University Press

Reed, M. (ed.) (2009) *Children and Language: Development, Impairment, and Training*. New York: Nova Science Publishers

Reed, S. (2010) *Thinking Visually*. New York: Psychology Press

Rees, A. and Palmer, A. (eds.) (2010) *The Oxford Handbook of Auditory Science: The Auditory Brain*. Oxford: Oxford University Press

Reisberg, D. (ed.) (2013) *The Oxford Handbook of Cognitive Psychology*. Oxford: Oxford University Press

Revlin, R. (2013) *Cognition: Theory and Practice*. New York: Worth Publishers

Riemer, N. (2010) *Introducing Semantics*. Cambridge: Cambridge University Press

Rieser, J. (ed.) (2008) *Blindness and Brain Plasticity in Navigation and Object Perception*. New York: Lawrence Erlbaum

Roach, P. (2001) *English Phonetics and Phonology*. Cambridge: Cambridge University Press

Rowsell, J. and Pahl, K. (eds.) (2015) *The Routledge Handbook of Literacy Studies*. London: Routledge

S

Sadato, N. (2005) 'How the blind 'see' Braille: Lessons from functional magnetic resonance imaging' *The Neuroscientist* 11: 577-582

Sadato, N., Okada, T., Honda, M. and Yonekura, Y. (2002) 'Critical period for cross-modal plasticity in blind humans: A functional MRI study' *NeuroImage* 16: 389-400

Sadato, N., Okada, T., Kubota, K. and Yonekura, Y. (2004) 'Tactile discrimination activates the visual cortex of the recently blind naïve to Braille: A functional magnetic resonance imaging study in humans' *Neuroscience Letters* 359: 49-52

Sadato, N., Pascual-Leone, A., Grafman, J., Deiber, M., Ibanez, V. and Hallett, M. (1998) 'Neural networks for Braille reading by the blind' *Brain* 121: 1213-1229

Salisbury, R. (ed.) (2008) *Teaching Pupils with Visual Impairment*. London: Routledge

Schiller, N. and Meyer, A. (eds.) (2003) *Phonetics and Phonology in Language Comprehension and Production*. Berlin: Mouton de Gruyter

Schmitt, N. (ed.) (2004) *Formulaic Sequences: Acquisition, Processing and Use*. Amsterdam: John Benjamins

Schnupp, J., Nelken, I. and King, A. (2011) *Auditory Neuroscience: Making Sense of Sound*. Cambridge: MIT Press

Schulkin, J. (2012) *Action, Perception and the Brain*. New York: Palgrave MacMillan

Sedlmeier, P. and Betsch, T. (2002) *ETC: Frequency Processing and Cognition*. Oxford: Oxford University Press

Sharwood Smith, M. and Truscott, J. (2014) *The Multilingual Mind: A Modular Processing Perspective*. Cambridge: Cambridge University Press

Shriberg, L. and Kent, R. (2013) *Clinical Phonetics* (4th edition). Boston: Pearson

Siegel, D. (2012) *The Developing Mind: How Relationships and the Brain Interact to Shape Who We Are (2nd edition)*. New York: Guilford Press

Siegel, S. (2010) *The Contents of Visual Experience*. Oxford: Oxford University Press

Silverman, R. and Hartranft, A. (2015) *Developing Vocabulary and Oral Language in Young Children*. New York: Guilford Press

Sinclair, J. (1987) *Looking Up: An Account of the COBUILD Project in Lexical Computing and the Development of the Collins COBUILD English Language Dictionary*. London: Collins ELT

Sinclair, J. (1991) *Corpus, Concordance, Collocation*. Oxford: Oxford University Press

Sloboda, J. (1985) *The Musical Mind: The Cognitive Psychology of Music*. Oxford: Oxford University Press

Smidt, S. (2009) *Planning for the Early Years Foundation Stage*. London: Routledge

Snowden, R., Thomson, P. and Troscianko, T. (2012) *Basic Vision: An Introduction to Visual Perception*. Oxford: Oxford University Press

Snyder, B. (2000) *Music and Memory: An Introduction*. Cambridge: MIT Press

Stein, B. (ed.) (2012) *The New Handbook of Multisensory Processes*. Cambridge: MIT Press

Stone, J. (2012) *Vision and Brain: How We Perceive the World*. Cambridge: MIT Press

Strange, W. (ed.) (1995) *Speech Perception and Linguistic Experience: Issues in Cross-Language Research*. Baltimore: York Press

T

Tan, S., Pforddresher, P. and Harre, R. (2010) *Psychology of Music: From Sound to Significance*. Hove: Psychology Press

Tarone, E., Bigelow, M. and Hansen, K. (2009) *Literacy and Second Language Oracy*. Oxford: Oxford University Press

Tatham, M. and Morton, K. (2006) *Speech Production and Perception*. London: Palgrave MacMillan

Tenbrink, T., Wiener, J. and Claramunt, C. (eds.) (2013) *Representing Space in Cognition: Interrelations of Behaviour, Language, and Formal Models*. Oxford: Oxford University Press

Tesar, B. (2014) *Output-Driven Phonology: Theory and Learning*. Cambridge: Cambridge University Press

Tobin, M. (1994) *Assessing Visually Handicapped People: An Introduction to Test Procedures*. London: David Fulton

Tobin, Y. (1997) *Phonology as Human Behavior: Theoretical Implications and Clinical Applications*. Durham: Duke University Press

Tohkura, Y., Vatikiotis-Bateson, E. and Sagisaka, Y. (eds.) (1992) *Speech Perception, Production, and Linguistic Structure*. Tokyo: Ohmsha

Treiman, R. and Kessler, B. (2014) *How Children Learn to Write Words*. Oxford: Oxford University Press

Trommer, J. (ed.) (2012) *The Morphology and Phonology of Exponence*. Oxford: Oxford University Press

Tsotsos, J. (2011) *A Computational Perspective on Visual Attention*. Cambridge: MIT Press

U

Unkelbach, C. and Greifeneder, R. (eds.) (2013) *The Experience of Thinking: How the Fluency of Mental Processes Influences Cognition and Behaviour*. London: Psychology Press

Upward, C. and Davidson, G. (2011) *The History of English Spelling*. Oxford: Wiley-Blackwell

V

van der Helm, P. (2014) *Simplicity in Vision: A Multidisciplinary Account of Perceptual Organization*. Cambridge: Cambridge University Press

Vihman, M. (2014) *Phonological Development: The First Two Years*. Oxford: Wiley-Blackwell

W

Wallin, N., Merker, B. and Brown, S. (eds.) (2000) *The Origin of Music*. Cambridge: MIT Press

Warren, D. (1984) *Blindness and Early Childhood Development (2nd edition)*. New York: American Foundation for the Blind

Warren, D. (1994) *Blindness and Children: An Individual Differences Approach*. Cambridge: Cambridge University Press

Warren, R. (2008) *Auditory Perception: An Analysis and Synthesis (3rd edition)*. Cambridge: Cambridge University Press

Webster, A. and Roe, J. (1998) *Children with Visual Impairments: Social Interaction, Language and Learning*. London: Routledge

Weiss, C., Gordon, M. and Lillywhite, H. (1987) *Clinical Management of Articulatory and Phonologic Disorders*. Baltimore: Williams & Wilkins

Wilcox, S. (1992) *The Phonetics of Fingerspelling*. Amsterdam: John Benjamins

Williams, M. (2012) *Perspectives on Diseases and Disorders: Speech Disorders*. Detroit: Gale

Wolfe, J., Kluender, K. and Levi, D. (2012) *Sensation & Perception (3rd edition)*. Sunderland: Sinauer Associates

Wolvin, A. (ed.) (2010) *Listening and Human Communication in* the 21st *Century*. Oxford: Wiley-Blackwell

Wood, D. (ed.) (2010) *Perspectives on Formulaic Language: Acquisition and Communication*. London: Continuum

Wood, D. (2012) *Formulaic Language and Second Language Speech Fluency: Background, Evidence and Classroom Applications*. London: Continuum

Wray, A. (2002) *Formulaic Language and the Lexicon*. Cambridge: Cambridge University Press

Wray, A. (2008) *Formulaic Language: Pushing the Boundaries*. Oxford: Oxford University Press

Y

Yavaş, M. (ed.) (1994) *First and Second Language Phonology*. San Diego: Singular Publishing

Yavaş, M. (2006) *Applied English Phonology*. Oxford: Blackwell

Yost, W. (2006) *Fundamentals of Hearing (5th edition)*. Bingley: Emerald

Z

Ziegler, W. and Deger, K. (eds.) (1998) *Clinical Phonetics and Linguistics*. London: Whurr Publishers

Index

A
absolute pitch   14, 113
acoustics   27
adapt   139
affricate   78, 86
aging   5, 52
alveolar   79
amplitude   7, 39
amusia   24
aphasia   24
apical-r   96
approximant   78
arbitrariness   232
articulation   103
aspiration   83
assimilation   47
attention   217, 221
audition   145, 267
auditory acuity   145
auditory attending   41
auditory attention span   41
auditory awareness   41
auditory blending   44
auditory closure   44
auditory cortex   150, 256
auditory discrimination   42
auditory memory   42
auditory memory span   43
auditory projection
    ability   43
auditory separation   43
auditory sequencing
    ability   43

B
baby talk   25
basilar membrane   6
bilabial   79
blind   2, 108, 141, 162, 199
Braille   145, 164, 169, 191, 196,
    234, 252, 277, 284
brightness   136
bunched-r   96

C
carry-over   118
categorised perception   36
category   202
chunk   228, 238, 270
clear-l   94
coarticulation   35, 36, 38, 51

cochlea   33, 52
cognition   236
collocation   271
communication   201, 226, 264
complex tone   9
comprehensibility   114
computer   61, 125, 152, 184, 274
concept   202
conceptual structure   192, 204
connected speech   48
consciousness   205
consonants   56, 77
context   240
contour   10
contraction   172
core cognition   211
Critical Period Hypothesis   113

D
dark-l   95
deaf   2
definition   208
dental   79
depth   137
discrimination   119
disparity   138

distance   137
dorsolateral temporal lobes   39
drills   61
dyad   25

E
ear training   121
echoic memory   8
emotion   156
English   55
events   6
explicit knowledge   212
explicit learning   113
exposure   53, 242
external feedback loop   128

F
face   138
feature analytic measurement   115
feedback   110, 130
feedforward   109, 130
filling-in process   37
flexibility   51
fluency   240, 273, 320
foreign accent   115, 154
formant   34, 57, 107
formulaic sequence   238
frequency   4, 33, 39, 240
fricative   77, 86

fundamental frequency   9, 40, 106

G
glide   78
gliding   94
glottal stop   80
Grade 1   172
Grade 2   172

H
haptic   141, 170, 189, 193, 236
hearing   255
hearing impairment   58
hearing loss   111, 129, 194
Hertz (Hz)   5
homograph   168
homophones   167

I
ideophone   232
image   203
imagery   191, 222
imitate   151
implicit learning   112
infant   151, 266
innate   211, 242
innateness   11
intelligibility   37, 114
intensity   7, 39
interaction   226
interference   113, 175

internal feedback loop   128
intuition   13

J
Japanese   55

K
Helen Keller   2

L
labiodental   79
larynx   106
learning   211, 249
left hemisphere   13, 27
lightness   136
lip reading   37, 151
liquid   78
listening   2, 31, 45, 225, 234, 255
literacy   164, 178, 307
localisation of sound   42
location   155
locomotion   218
long-term memory   32
loudness   7
luminance   136

M
manner   77, 107
maximal opposition   60
McGurk effect   150
meaning   205
melody   8, 27, 30

mental image   144
mental imagery   147
mental representation   202
minimal pair   60
monitor   127
mora   49
motion   139
motor cortex   104
motor development   223
multimodal   153, 190

N
nasal   79
noise   37

O
object   139
onomatopoeia   232

P
palatal   80
palatoalveolar   80
perception   236
perceptual assimilation   47
perceptual error   184
perceptual learning   53
perceptual magnet   47
Perkins Braille Writer   180
phonation   106
phoneme   107, 163
phonetics   32
phonics   284, 312
phonological awareness   162, 171, 267
phonological encoding   127
phonology   32, 117
photoreceptor   137
pitch   5, 30, 106
place   79, 107
plasticity   16, 28, 52, 191
plosive   77, 82
pointing   226
presbycusis   194
primary visual cortex   135
prosody   19, 26, 48

R
reaction time   315
reading   161, 267, 279
re-auditorisation   44
recency   240
recording   261
relative pitch   14
representation   133, 202
respiration   105
retrography   185
rhythm   18, 27, 30
rhythmic grouping   10
right hemisphere   13, 27

S
segmentation   48
self-monitoring   127

sensation   4, 236
sensitive   299
sensitive ears   3
sensitivity   47, 196, 217
sensory compensation   145, 217
sequence   8
short-term memory   11
sine wave   9
sinusoid   9
sound   4
space   140
spatial structure   204, 221
spectrogram   39, 108
spectrograph   39, 107
speed   255
spelling   166, 284, 308
stimulus   4
stress   49
stylus   180
syllable   19, 104

T
tactile   112, 145, 170, 193, 217, 236, 277
tactual   236
thought   207
timbre   7, 10, 27, 28, 30
time   18
token   204

tone   9
tongue height   56
tongue position   56
tongue shape   56
touch   144, 170, 189, 193, 217, 223, 236, 277, 314
transcription measure   115
tuning   33
turn-taking   226
type   204
typing   180

U
unvoiced   80

V
velar   80
ventriloquism effect   149
verbalism   220, 230
vibration   4
vision   133
visual cortex   144, 190
visual feedback   61, 126
visual information   37
vocal cord   40
vocal fold   106
vocal tract   36, 38, 106
voice   105, 129
voiced   80
vowels   56

W

what pathway   140
where pathway   140
word processing   183
word recognition   32, 234
working memory   239, 313
writing   179

【著者紹介】

中森誉之（なかもり たかゆき）

〈学歴〉横浜国立大学教育学部中学校教員養成課程英語科（学士）、ロンドン大学大学院音声学・言語学研究科（言語学修士）、東京学芸大学大学院連合学校教育学研究科（教育学博士）。
〈職歴〉日本学術振興会特別研究員、横浜国立大学非常勤講師を経て、現在京都大学大学院人間・環境学研究科准教授。

〈主要著書〉 *Chunking and Instruction: The Place of Sounds, Lexis, and Grammar in English Language Teaching*（2009 ひつじ書房）、『学びのための英語学習理論』（2009 ひつじ書房）、『学びのための英語指導理論』（2010 ひつじ書房）、『外国語はどこに記憶されるのか』（2013 開拓社）、『外国語音声の認知メカニズム』（2016 開拓社）

本書刊行にあたっては、JSPS科研費 JP16HP5216の助成を受けた。
This publication was supported by JSPS KAKENHI Grant Number JP16HP5216.

Foreign Language Learning without Vision
Sound Perception, Speech Production, and Braille
Takayuki Nakamori

発行	2016年10月10日 初版1刷
定価	8000円＋税
著者	Ⓒ 中森誉之
発行者	松本功
装丁者	大崎善治
印刷所	三美印刷株式会社
製本所	株式会社 星共社
発行所	株式会社 ひつじ書房
	〒112-0011 東京都文京区千石2-1-2 大和ビル2階
	Tel.03-5319-4916 Fax.03-5319-4917
	郵便振替 00120-8-142852
	toiawase@hituzi.co.jp　http://www.hituzi.co.jp/
	ISBN978-4-89476-828-4

造本には充分注意しておりますが、落丁・乱丁などがございましたら、小社かお買上げ書店にておとりかえいたします。ご意見、ご感想など、小社までお寄せ下されば幸いです。

刊行のご案内

Chunking and Instruction: The Place of Sounds, Lexis, and Grammar in English Language Teaching
Takayuki Nakamori 著　定価 8,800 円＋税

学びのための英語学習理論—つまずきの克服と指導への提案
中森誉之著　定価 2,400 円＋税

学びのための英語指導理論—4 技能の指導方法とカリキュラム設計の提案
中森誉之著　定価 2,600 円＋税

刊行のご案内

Metaphor of Emotions in English: With Special Reference to the Natural World and the Animal Kingdom as Their Source Domains
Ayako Omori 著　定価 9,500 円＋税

On Peripheries: Exploring Clause Initial and Clause Final Positions
Anna Cardinaletti, Guglielmo Cinque and Yoshio Endo 編　定価 14,000 円＋税

A Contrastive Study of Responsibility for Understanding Utterances between Japanese and Korean
Sumi Yoon 著　定価 8,400 円＋税

刊行のご案内

Relational Practice in Meeting Discourse in New Zealand and Japan
Kazuyo Murata 著　定価 6,000 円 + 税

Style and Creativity: Towards a Theory of Creative Stylistics
Saito Yoshifumi 著　定価 7,500 円 + 税